THE RACE FOR SPACE

THE RACE FOR SPACE

The United States and the Soviet Union Compete for the New Frontier

Betsy Kuhn

TWENTY-FIRST CENTURY BOOKS · MINNEAPOLIS

To My Mom

Author Acknowledgments
I would like to thank the following people for their help on this book: Edwinna Bernat; everyone in DTG, especially Marty Reid; Mark Gochnour and the staff of the Poolesville, Maryland, Public Library; and my three favorite Earthlings, G.K., M.K. and N.K.—B.K.

A Word about Metric Conversions, Spelling, Grammar, and Song
Metric conversions have not been included in quotations to preserve their authenticity. (Visit http://www.metrics.com for easy conversions.) For the same reason, the original spelling and grammar of primary sources have been retained. Chapter titles are fitting songs, popular during the space race era.

Twenty-First Century Books
A division of Lerner Publishing Group
241 First Avenue North
Minneapolis, Minnesota 55401 U.S.A.

Website address: www.lernerbooks.com

Library of Congress Cataloging-in-Publication Data

Kuhn, Betsy.
     The race for space / by Betsy Kuhn.
       p.   cm. — (People's history)
     Includes bibliographical references and index.
     ISBN-13: 978–0–8225–5984–9 (lib. bdg. : alk. paper)
     ISBN-10: 0–8225–5984–6 (lib. bdg. : alk. paper)
       1. Space race—United States—History—Juvenile literature. 2. Space race—Soviet Union—History—Juvenile literature. 3. Astronautics—United States—History—Juvenile literature. 4. Astronautics—Soviet Union—History—Juvenile literature. I. Title. II. Series.
TL793.K84 2007
629.45'009—dc22   200401791

Manufactured in the United States of America
1 2 3 4 5 6 – JR – 12 11 10 09 08 07

Contents

A couple listens to news of Soviet satellite *Sputnik* on a radio *(left)*.

"Wake Up Little Susie"

By Monday morning, almost every word on the radio was about Sputnik.

—youngster Homer H. Hickam Jr., on the 1957 launch and orbit of the Soviet satellite Sputnik (Rocket Boys, 1998)

It was Friday evening in the United States, October 4, 1957. That night a new TV show named *Leave It to Beaver* was making its debut. In the first episode, second-grader Beaver Cleaver was worried because his teacher had given him a note for his parents. Surely, it must mean something bad.

While Beaver's fears played out on TV screens across the United States, the country's fears were coming true in the sky above them. That day the Soviets (Russians) had launched a satellite into Earth's orbit. No one had ever done that before. And the Soviet Union, the United States' number one enemy, had been first.

A ten-year-old boy named Stephen King found out at the movies. He was at the local theater watching *Earth vs. the Flying Saucers*. This was his kind of movie, all about aliens who wanted to take over Earth.

Suddenly the film stopped. The house lights came on. The house manager appeared and held up his hands for silence. The Soviets, he announced, had launched an Earth satellite. It was named *Sputnik*, and it was at that very moment orbiting Earth. "This news remembered King was "greeted by absolute, tomblike silence."

Science-fiction movies, such as *Earth vs. the Flying Saucers*, played to people's curiosity and fear about space. In 1957 the Soviet Union made the exploration of space real, successfully launching the satellite *Sputnik 1*.

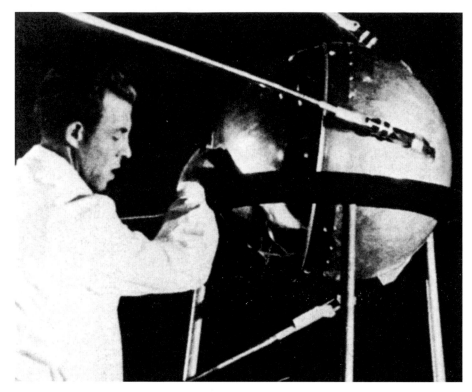

A Soviet scientist works on *Sputnik 1.* In 1957 the satellite became the first man-made object to orbit Earth. The U.S.-Soviet race for space was on.

Aliens were pretend. The Russians, on the other hand, were real. Now they were right overhead, or at least, their satellite was.

Homer H. Hickam Jr., a teenager in West Virginia, heard about *Sputnik* Saturday morning on the radio. Usually the local station played rock and roll. But that morning, Hickam remembered, "what I heard on the radio was a steady beep-beep-beep sound." The tone, said the announcer, was from *Sputnik.*

Hickam, a space enthusiast, knew immediately that *Sputnik* was an Earth satellite. What's more, he knew that the Americans were working on launching one too. "I can't believe the Russians beat us to it!" he exclaimed.

"Will it fly over America?" asked his mom.

When Homer replied that it probably would, she said, "If it does, it's going to upset your dad no end."

Sputnik, in fact, did upset lots of dads, moms, and other people. The satellite was a 184-pound (83-kilogram) sphere, 23 inches (58 centimeters) in diameter, just a radio transmitter in a small metal orb. Its name, which means "fellow traveler" in Russian, couldn't have been more harmless. But it set off one of the most exciting races in the history of humankind, the race for space. Who would be first to put someone on the Moon, the Americans or the Russians?

Duck and Cover

"When I was growing up in Dearborn, Michigan, there was a billboard on the main road near my house," remembers Rose Gottemoeller of the Carnegie Endowment for International Peace. "It showed a happy family gathered around their father as he cheerily read a newspaper in a comfortable chair. 'Let us build your bomb shelter for you,' the billboard read. 'So many uses in peacetime! Dad's den! Mom's sewing room!'"

U.S. schoolchildren duck beneath their desks during a safety drill in the 1950s. The duck-and-cover technique was intended to increase students' chances of surviving missile and bomb attacks.

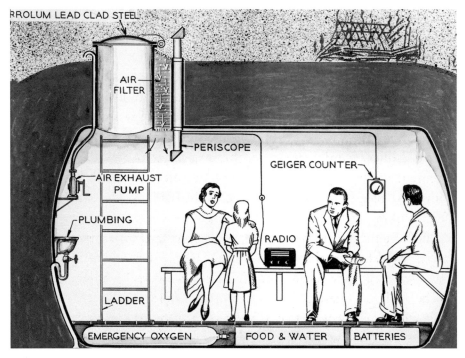

RROLUM LEAD CLAD STEEL

AIR FILTER

PERISCOPE

GEIGER COUNTER

AIR EXHAUST PUMP

PLUMBING

RADIO

LADDER

EMERGENCY OXYGEN | FOOD & WATER | BATTERIES

This 1950s diagram shows an American family safe in a bomb shelter after a hypothetical Soviet nuclear attack. But no one was sure how long families would have to stay underground or if there would be a society to return to.

She also remembered the "duck-and-cover" drills at school. If a bomb hit the school, she and the other students were to go "out into the hallway, sit down, back to lockers, head between knees; or, under desk, curl up, forehead to floor."

A bomb? Yes. In case the Russians bombed the United States. Communists, who believe that wealth and power should belong to the working people, had taken over the Russian government in the early 1900s and used government control to enforce their ideas. The new name for the country —and other states under its control—was the Union of Soviet Socialist Republics, or Soviet Union, and it seemed poised to spread its power around the globe. In 1949 the Soviets had tested their first successful nuclear bomb. A nuclear bomb was many times more deadly than a conventional one. It killed through an explosion and radiation. It seemed entirely possible that the Russians could strike the United States.

Bill Bradley, who became a professional basketball player and then a U.S. senator, remembers designing his ideal bomb shelter as a kid. "I identified where I was going to put my cot, where I was going to put my favorite books and where I was going to put my basketball."

Pam Miller's family stockpiled food, such as peanut butter, in the basement of their home in Ferguson, Missouri. "I remember my dad filling old bleach bottles with water," she said, so the family would have drinking water.

But for all the fear, most citizens found it hard to believe the Soviet Union could be superior to the United States. They imagined Russia as a backward country full of poor farmers and women in head scarves.

The United States, on the other hand, offered all the modern conveniences anyone could want. There were shiny new cars, refrigerator-freezers, dandy new barbecue grills. Surely such a country would lead the world in technological achievement.

Panic

Day after day, *Sputnik* orbited Earth. The word *Sputnik* "was like 'bread,'" said Pam Miller. "Everyone knew it."

In some places, it was even possible to see *Sputnik*, or at least the third stage or section of the rocket that bore it, at dawn and dusk. Dexter Stegemeyer, who lived outside of Fairbanks, Alaska, was the first person in the Western Hemisphere to see it. He was sitting in his outhouse with the door open early on the morning of October 6, 1957, when he saw *Sputnik* fly past. A plaque commemorates Stegemeyer's outhouse sighting.

R. Mike Mullane, who grew up to be an astronaut, remembers his neighbors in Albuquerque, New Mexico, gathering in their front yards to catch a glimpse of *Sputnik* in the evening sky. "It was like Halloween," he said. "A tiny light appeared on the southwestern horizon and slowly, silently glided over our heads." He remembers, "People stood in awe. Some cried. Some were frightened."

"Soon [the Russians] will be dropping bombs on us from space like kids dropping rocks onto cars from freeway overpasses," warned Senator Lyndon B. Johnson of Texas.

The notion that the Russians were a bunch of peasant farmers disappeared. Their children, it was said, studied longer hours than American children. Soviet science and math courses were much more advanced. In fact, when Homer Hickam Jr. turned on the radio the Monday after *Sputnik*'s launch, the disc jockey was urging students to study hard to "catch up with the Russians." He played the *beep-beep-beep* of *Sputnik* over and over. "It seemed as if he thought if he played us his usual rock and roll, we might get even farther behind the Russian kids," remembers Hickam.

In Washington, D.C., *Sputnik* had the nation's leaders in an uproar. "The only other time that I remember there being such an impact [in the capital] was when the atomic bomb went off," said Eilene Galloway of the Legislative Reference Service.

Congress was not meeting at the time, but many people urged President Dwight D. Eisenhower to call the legislators back into a special session. President Eisenhower refused. He was not about to be rattled by *Sputnik*. In fact, he waited a full five days, until October 9, 1957, to even hold a press conference.

Normally the press corps was friendly and respectful to the popular president. But not that day.

"Mr. President, Russia has launched an Earth satellite," began reporter Merriman Smith. "I ask you, sir, what are we going to do about it?" One after another, the reporters hurled questions at Eisenhower.

The president remained calm. The fact that the Soviets "have put one small ball in the air" concerned him "not one iota." The United States, he reminded them, planned to launch its own satellite in 1958. The country's satellite program was strictly scientific and "never has been considered as a race."

He had a point. World scientists had designated 1958 as the International Geophysical Year, or IGY. During the IGY, scientists the world over would work to learn more about Earth and space and make their findings available to all. In 1955 the United States had announced that it would launch a satellite during the IGY. The Soviets, soon after, announced that they, too, would put up a satellite. But their announcement went mostly unnoticed.

"Shaggiest, Lonesomest Dog"

Premier Nikita Khrushchev, the Soviet Union's leader, was delighted that his scientists' shiny little satellite had put the world into such a frenzy. The fortieth anniversary of the Russian Revolution, the birth of the Soviet Union, was coming up. Khrushchev instructed his space engineers to commemorate the event with another astounding feat.

On November 3, 1957, the Soviets launched a new satellite. This one was a whopping 1,118 pounds (507 kg). It was so big that in the *New York Times*, scientists speculated that the Soviets would soon "detonate a nuclear bomb on the Moon."

But its huge size was not all that distinguished *Sputnik 2*. It also carried the first living passenger

A Soviet rocket stands poised on the launchpad just before sending *Sputnik 2* —and a passenger—into Earth's orbit in November 1957.

into space, a small mutt named Laika with trusting brown eyes. There was just one problem. Although the Soviets knew how to put Laika into space, they did not yet know how to bring her safely down. Laika was doomed to die in space.

The fate of poor Laika provoked worldwide outrage. Animal lovers picketed the United Nations (an international peace-keeping organization) on behalf of the "shaggiest, lonesomest, saddest dog in all history," as the *New York Times* referred to Laika.

But why had the Soviets launched a dog? The answer was clear: they were preparing to send a man into space. While Laika lived, the Soviets monitored her heartbeat and other vital functions. Knowing how a dog fared in space would help them understand how a human would react.

"Flopnik"

Many Americans were getting impatient. They wondered why it was taking so long for their country to launch a satellite.

Actually, the United States already had developed the necessary rocket technology. It's just that the wrong people had come up with the technology. The army's Redstone Arsenal in Huntsville, Alabama, under the direction of German-born scientist Wernher von Braun, had developed a powerful Jupiter-C rocket that would have worked just fine.

But the satellite program was supposed to be strictly a scientific endeavor, not a military one. And in 1957, there was no NASA (National Aeronautics and Space Administration). The program had been assigned to the Naval Research Laboratory, but the program was under the control of the National Science Foundation. This was the program, named Vanguard, that was to launch a satellite in 1958 for the International Geophysical Year.

But the pressure created by the Soviet satellites was so intense that the U.S. naval team announced it would make a test launch in early

December. On December 6, 1957, reporters and photographers crowded into Cocoa Beach, Florida, near the Cape Canaveral launch site. They set up cameras on the roofs of motels and on the beach. The whole United States was watching for the navy to restore the country's sense of pride.

The Vanguard rocket rose a few feet from the launchpad. Then it slid back down, crumpled, and burst into flames. Its little satellite, no bigger than a grapefruit, rolled off to the side of the launchpad and obediently began to beep.

"OH WHAT A FLOPNIK!" announced one newspaper. "Kaputnik!" said others. A popular joke asked, "What will Americans find on the Moon?" The answer: Russians.

Move Over, *Sputnik!*

After the launch of *Sputnik 2*, the Eisenhower administration allowed von Braun and his team at the Redstone Arsenal to move forward with their satellite program. On January 31, 1958, under von Braun's direction, the army launched a 31-pound (14 kg) satellite, named *Explorer 1*, into orbit using a Jupiter-C rocket. The rocket launch went fine, but would the satellite reach orbit? Ninety minutes after

A Jupiter-C rocket roars from the launchpad in Huntsville, Alabama, on January 31, 1958. It sent the *Explorer 1* satellite into orbit around Earth.

the launch, the Goldstone tracking station in California reported, "Goldstone has the bird." *Explorer 1* was in orbit!

The residents of Huntsville, Alabama, where the rocket had been made, jammed the streets, honking their horns. They waved placards saying, "Move Over *Sputnik!* Space is Ours."

In Coalwood, West Virginia, Homer Hickam Jr. watched the launch on TV with his friends. His buddy O'Dell Carroll "got up and did a little jig, and then fell back on the couch and put his feet up in the air like he was riding a bicycle," Hickam remembers. "I felt proud and patriotic."

The United States had reached space at last. Even so, Americans felt that the country was far behind the Soviet Union in the space race, that is, the race to conquer space through technology. They spoke of a missile gap between the two countries.

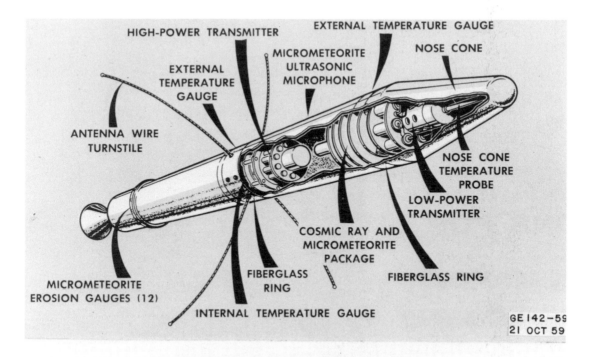

HIGH-POWER TRANSMITTER

EXTERNAL TEMPERATURE GAUGE

MICROMETEORITE ULTRASONIC MICROPHONE

NOSE CONE

EXTERNAL TEMPERATURE GAUGE

ANTENNA WIRE TURNSTILE

NOSE CONE TEMPERATURE PROBE

LOW-POWER TRANSMITTER

COSMIC RAY AND MICROMETEORITE PACKAGE

MICROMETEORITE EROSION GAUGES (12)

FIBERGLASS RING

FIBERGLASS RING

INTERNAL TEMPERATURE GAUGE

GE 142-59
21 OCT 59

EXPLORER I

This diagram shows the parts of U.S. satellite *Explorer 1*. The satellite collected and sent data to NASA, which led to the first major discovery of the space race—the Van Allen radiation belts around Earth.

But how had this happened? The United States was the most powerful and advanced country in the world. How had the Soviet Union bested it?

One popular explanation was that Americans had become too preoccupied with inventing a better car, a better refrigerator, a better TV show. Look what the country had "launched" the night the Soviets put up *Sputnik: Leave It to Beaver*!

Many people blamed the educational system. The United States needed to stress science and math in its schools, as the Soviets did.

It was time for the country to make some changes.

"High Hopes"

The country was wild with space fever!

—R. Mike Mullane, recalling excitement
over the race for space in the United States during the late 1950s

In March 1958, *Life* magazine introduced its readers to two teenage boys. Sixteen-year-old Stephen Lapekas of Chicago, Illinois, was a smart kid. But his grades, said *Life,* were mediocre. Stephen wasn't particularly concerned. "I worry about 'em," he said, "but that's about as far as it goes." Even in Typing II, he joked, he could only "type about a word a minute."

Then there was Alexei Kutzkov, also sixteen, of the Soviet Union. Alexei attended school six days a week. His classes included advanced physics, chemistry, and electrical technique. For Alexei, grades were a primary concern for he was "filled with a fierce determination to get to college and become a physicist." Fun—usually a game of chess—came only "after his long homework chores are over," said *Life*.

The issue was called the "Crisis in Education." Schools in the United States were "in terrible shape," said one article. There were too many students like Stephen, doing just enough to get by, and far too few like Alexei, eager to wring every drop of knowledge from their schooling. Science courses in U.S. schools, the article alleged, were few and not as advanced as those the Soviets offered. What's more, ten million Soviet students were studying English. As for U.S. students, just over 15 percent of them even studied a foreign language.

Warned writer Sloan Wilson, "The outcome of the arms race will depend eventually on our schools and those of the Russians." In other words, if its schools didn't shape up, the United States could face an unthinkable fate: it would lose the Cold War (1945–1991).

The cover of the March 24, 1958, *Life* magazine issue was dedicated to the "crisis in education." The issue explored problems in U.S. education by contrasting Soviet student Alexei Kutzkov and U.S. student Stephen Lapekas.

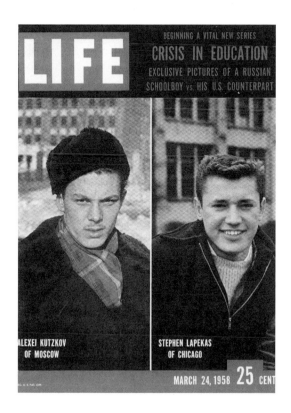

The Cold War had started with the end of World War II (1939–1945). The United States and Great Britain, allies during the war, worked hard to make such countries as West Germany, a former enemy, strong and democratic. But the Soviet Union, which was also a World War II ally, simply took over the Eastern European countries it occupied at the war's end. They became Communist countries, trapped behind what British prime minister Winston Churchill called an Iron Curtain.

Since the close of World War II, the United States and the Soviet Union had been enemies. Both were striving to become the dominant world power. The United States was proud of its capitalist, democratic system. The Soviet Union promoted Communism.

In 1949 the Cold War took an ominous step forward when the Soviet Union successfully tested an atomic bomb. Until then, only the United States had been able to explode such a bomb. Suddenly, the world's two biggest superpowers had the ability to destroy each other.

When the North Koreans, who were Communists, invaded non-Communist South Korea in the early fifties, U.S. troops were sent in to help the South. In the Korean War (1950–1953), which lasted approximately three years, U.S. troops helped to push back the North Koreans. In the end, Korea remained divided into Communist North Korea and non-Communist South Korea, just as it had been before the war.

Lots of people in the United States were nervous about Communism. U.S. senator Joseph McCarthy of Wisconsin and the House Un-American Activities Committee wrongly accused thousands of citizens of being loyal to the Communists. These people were blacklisted, or added to lists of suspected Communists. They lost their jobs. Many employers refused to hire them, and blacklisted citizens found it nearly impossible to find work. Some were jailed for refusing to identify colleagues and friends with Communist ties.

Loyalty oaths became common. In the mid-fifties, Edwinna Bernat was just starting her career as an elementary schoolteacher in western

Pennsylvania. Nothing about her background suggested she was a threat to democracy. Still, she had to take an oath declaring loyalty to the United States before she could sign the contract for her first teaching job.

Educational Emergency

President Eisenhower had said the Sputnik program concerned him "not one iota." Nonetheless, the satellite spurred him to make some fast changes. He appointed the nation's first national science adviser, naming Dr. James R. Killian Jr., president of the Massachusetts Institute of Technology (MIT), to the post.

The president also established the Advanced Research Projects Agency (ARPA) within the department of defense. ARPA would oversee all advanced research projects within the defense department, regardless of whether they were navy, army, air force, or marine projects. Such an agency "would have been unthinkable without Sputnik because [ARPA] cut across all the services," noted Willis H. Shapley, who served with the U.S. Bureau of the Budget.

But the biggest changes came in education. Throughout the nation's history, the U.S. government had largely stayed out of education. According to Stewart McClure, then the chief clerk of the Senate Committee on Labor, Education, and Public Welfare, many people felt "that the last thing that could happen in the United States was for the federal hand to be laid on local education." Most Americans felt strongly that control of education should be left to local governments. They would "scream and wave their hands in the air about the *horrible* prospects of this vicious, cold hand of federal bureaucracy being laid upon these pristine, splendid local schools."

Even so, many people in the U.S. government were eager to try to improve education. The *Sputnik* scare gave them their chance.

"An educational emergency exists and requires action by the federal government," began the National Defense Education Act of 1958.

The act authorized millions of dollars of loans to college students to study science, math, and foreign languages. It funded the increased use of audiovisual equipment such as educational television and film projectors in the classroom. Funding for school guidance counselors was also increased so that counselors might identify able students and encourage them to attend college.

In addition, Congress authorized huge budget increases for the National Science Foundation. The foundation, in turn, funded the development of new math and science curricula. Edwinna Bernat remembers receiving a lot of exciting, hands-on materials for her fifth-grade students.

The country's top scientists stepped in to help elementary and secondary schools. "Nobel laureates sought ways to teach the very young how scientists and mathematicians think," notes Peter Dow, author of *Schoolhouse Politics: Lessons from the Sputnik Era*. Physicist Jerrold Zacharias of the Massachusetts Institute of Technology, for instance, had been urging an overhaul of the high school physics curriculum even before *Sputnik 1*. Once *Sputnik 1* went up, people were ready to listen to him. He brought together scientists to create new textbooks, laboratory kits, films, and more to bring the physics curriculum into the modern age.

What's more, many school systems were working hard to catch up with the Soviets. Some extended their school days. Ocean City, New Jersey, schools held advanced science and math classes on Saturdays. Others held evening classes, and at a junior high school in Fair Lawn, New Jersey, ninety seventh graders signed up for Russian language classes.

Have Rocket—Will Travel

Perhaps the government needn't have worried about U.S. students falling behind the Soviets. All across the country, the satellite launches had inspired young citizens to reach for the stars. Homer

A youth prepares his model rocket for launch in the late 1950s. Space fever excited kids—and adults—in the United States. Many took up model rocketry. Clubs and even national associations formed around the popular hobby.

H. Hickam Jr. was one of them. The day after the launch of *Explorer 1*, he gathered his friends in his bedroom in Coalwood, West Virginia.

"Okay, here's what we're going to do," he said. He and his buddies were "going to learn all there was about rockets and start building them." They'd form a rocket club called the Big Creek Missile Agency. For the sake of their rockets, Hickam and his friends began studying advanced subjects like trigonometry all on their own.

In Austin, Minnesota, the teenaged members of the Austin Rocket Society were so inspired by *Sputnik 2* that they launched a fifty-cent mouse 1,642 feet (500 meters) into the air at 221 miles per hour (356 kilometers per hour). The mouse, stowed in the wooden nose cone, did not survive. (The local humane society pressed charges against the boys, but they were eventually dropped.) At the 1958 science fair in Morehead City, North Carolina, the theme was "Have Rocket—Will Travel." The fair featured rocket launchings every half hour.

"The country was wild with space fever!" said R. Mike Mullane. "The Boy Scouts started a space merit badge. Toy companies started selling model kits of satellites and rockets. Schools had space days." Suddenly, regular folks were talking about rocket science. "It's not rocket science," went the new saying, which meant, "It's simple, really."

NASA and the Mercury Seven

Hickam had it easy forming the Big Creek Missile Agency. He simply gathered his friends in his bedroom, and the BCMA was a going thing. Establishing a national rocket and space agency was more complicated.

"The Air Force felt that it should be the agency to do all space research," remembered Paul G. Dembling, the former legal representative for NASA. But "the Atomic Energy Commission felt very strongly that, if we were going to go into space, nuclear power was going to put us there, and therefore it should be the agency to assume that role." And, of course, the army's Redstone Arsenal, where Wernher von Braun and his team were developing rockets like the one that had launched the *Explorer 1*, seemed a logical candidate, too.

What's more, space was clearly an international subject. "Right away we needed international tracking stations," recalled Eilene Galloway of the Legislative Reference Service. "Satellites went around the globe," traveling over national boundaries. The State Department would need to be involved as well.

Dr. Killian, President Eisenhower's science adviser, convinced the president that the new agency should be a civilian one, not a military agency. The exploration of space was to be a peaceful enterprise, after all.

Thus, on October 1, 1958, the National Aeronautics and Space Administration, known as NASA, was established as a civilian agency. Its "activities in space should be devoted to peaceful purposes for the benefit of all mankind," said the Space Act of 1958. The core of NASA's staff came from the civilian agency known as NACA, the National Advisory Committee for Aeronautics.

NASA's first undertaking would be Project Mercury. In this multi-year, multistep program, the agency would put a number of manned spacecraft in orbit around Earth, safely recover them, and evaluate the effects of spaceflight on the person involved.

By this time, even President Eisenhower had caught the space bug. In December 1958, he delivered a tape-recorded Christmas message via the world's first communications satellite. Project SCORE had launched a satellite on December 18 that could transmit prerecorded messages.

"This is the President of the United States speaking," he said. "My voice is coming to you from a satellite traveling in outer space. My message is a simple one: Through this unique means I convey to you and all mankind, America's wish for peace on Earth and goodwill toward men everywhere."

In April 1959, the news from the world of space was even more exciting. NASA introduced the United States's first seven astronauts—known as the Mercury Seven. (Their Soviet

The Mercury Seven. *(From left to right at front)* Walter M. "Wally" Schirra Jr., Donald K. "Deke" Slayton, John H. Glenn Jr., and M. Scott Carpenter. (From *left to right at back)* Alan B. Shepard Jr., Virgil I. "Gus" Grissom Jr., and L. Gordon Cooper Jr.

rivals were called cosmonauts, from the Russian word *kosmonavt.)* The seven were Alan B. Shepard, Donald K. "Deke" Slayton, Virgil I. "Gus" Grissom, John H. Glenn, Scott Carpenter, L. Gordon Cooper Jr., and Walter M. "Wally" Schirra. They had been carefully selected from among the nation's top military test pilots. All were white, handsome, and all-American looking, and every one of them was an instant hero. People couldn't get enough of them. Americans wanted to know about the astronauts' wives and kids, what foods they liked, what sports they liked, what cars they drove, *everything.*

If Americans had been excited about space before the astronauts hit the scene, now they were even more so. Suddenly, kids all over the United States wanted to be astronauts too. R. Mike Mullane dreamed he would be the first American in space. "I even stopped drinking milk shakes to stay light," he said.

Senator Hillary Rodham Clinton of New York was eleven at the time. "I wrote to NASA to volunteer for astronaut training," she remembered. "I received a letter back informing me that they were not accepting girls in the program." She was outraged.

A young woman named Shannon Lucid was so angry that the astronauts were all male that she sent a letter to *Time* magazine. Lucid had been interested in space since before *Sputnik 1.* In school she had told her teacher that she wanted to be a rocket scientist. The teacher replied that there was no such thing as rocket scientists, and if there were, they wouldn't be women.

Lagging Behind

The United States had a space agency, seven dashing astronauts, and a president who delivered holiday cheer via satellite. Even so, the country still lagged behind the Soviet Union. In July 1959, Vice President Richard Nixon debated Soviet premier Khrushchev in Moscow. "There are some instances where you may be ahead of us," the vice president conceded to Khrushchev, "for example, in the development

U.S. vice president Richard Nixon *(front right)* forcefully challenges Soviet leader Nikita Khrushchev *(front left)* and his ideas about Russian superiority during the 1959 Kitchen Debate in Moscow, the Soviet capital.

of the thrust of your rockets." But, he noted, in other ways "we are ahead of you." For instance, the United States had "many different kinds of washing machines so that the housewives have a choice."

Khrushchev was unimpressed. The American goods were "merely gadgets," he replied. As if to prove his point, that September the Soviets became the first country to successfully crash-land a lunar probe (a collection of rocket-propelled scientific instruments) on the Moon. NASA had launched a number of lunar probes too, but none had yet touched the Moon.

That same year, there was Cold War news of a far more serious nature. Just 90 miles (145 km) south of Florida, in the island country of Cuba, Communist leader Fidel Castro had come into power. Not only was this nearby neighbor an ally of the Soviet Union, Cuba was also close enough to easily serve as a launch site for a missile strike on the United States.

A New Frontier

In the United States, 1960 was a presidential election year. That spring Homer Hickam Jr. was visiting Welch, West Virginia, to shop for a suit. His Big Creek Missile Agency had won first place in the state science fair with its entry on rocketry techniques. Homer was going to attend the National Science Fair in Indianapolis, Indiana, and he needed something nice to wear.

That afternoon Senator John F. Kennedy of Massachusetts, a Democratic candidate for president, made a campaign stop in Welch. Homer strolled over to hear his speech. When the senator asked for questions, Homer raised his hand.

"What do you think the United States ought to do in space?" he asked Senator Kennedy.

"What do *you* think we ought to do in space?" Kennedy returned the question.

Presidential hopeful John F. Kennedy *(right)* addresses a crowd while on the campaign trail in 1960. The U.S. space program was important to Kennedy, and he made it part of his political platform.

An Echo satellite undergoes testing in 1960. The metallic balloon Echo satellites were massive, measuring 100 feet (30 meters) in diameter (see car at bottom center for scale). The satellites worked by reflecting communication signals sent from one point on Earth to another.

"We should go to the Moon," answered Homer.

Some people laughed. Not Kennedy. "I like what this young man says," he said. "The important thing is to get this country going again. . . . If going to the Moon can help us do that, then maybe that's what we should do."

That summer Kennedy won the Democratic nomination for president. "These are entirely new times and they require new solutions," he said. He captured citizens' imaginations by speaking of space as the New Frontier. "High hopes, we've got high hopes," went his theme song.

In August the United States made a huge step toward the New Frontier. It launched what looked like an immense lightweight silver balloon called *Echo 1*. *Echo 1*, which inflated upon reaching space, was the first communications satellite that could both receive and send a signal in real time. (The SCORE satellite launched in 1958

The Soviet Union sent Strelka *(left)* and Belka *(right)* into space aboard *Sputnik 5* on August 19, 1960. They, along with forty mice, two rats, and several plants, returned safely to Earth after spending one day in orbit.

could only transmit prerecorded signals.) On August 18, *Echo 1* successfully transmitted a message from New Jersey to France. At the time, people had to rely on telephone and telegraph cables to communicate across oceans. *Echo 1* led the way for modern sophisticated satellite communications.

One day later, the Soviets reached a milestone of their own. They launched *Sputnik 5* with two dogs, Belka and Strelka, aboard. Unlike poor Laika, these dogs were brought safely back to Earth in their craft via parachute. The Soviets, then, had been the first to launch a live creature into space and return it to Earth.

That fall the presidential campaign dominated the news. Kennedy's Republican opponent was Vice President Richard M. Nixon. The Cold War was a major issue in the race. "For the first time in our history," said Kennedy, referring to Cuba, "an enemy stands at the throat of the United States." There was a "missile gap," he claimed, between the Soviets and the Americans. "I will take my television in black and white," he told an audience in Oklahoma City. "I want to be ahead of them in rocket thrust." And at the Do Drop Inn, in Muskegon, Michigan, he spoke of his concern that "the first dogs carried around in outer space were not named Rover and Fido, but, instead, were named Belka and Strelka."

In November 1960, U.S. voters elected John F. Kennedy by a narrow margin to be the next president. The country, it seemed, was ready to venture with him into the New Frontier.

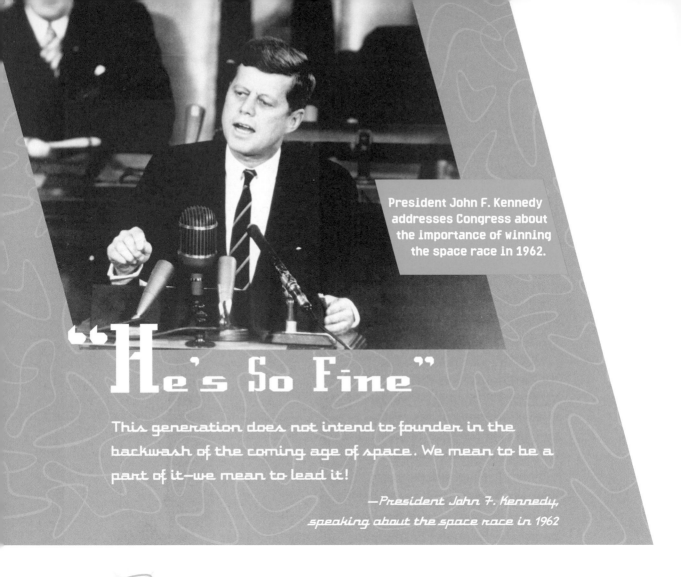

President John F. Kennedy addresses Congress about the importance of winning the space race in 1962.

"He's So Fine"

This generation does not intend to founder in the backwash of the coming age of space. We mean to be a part of it—we mean to lead it!

—President John F. Kennedy, speaking about the space race in 1962

On January 20, 1961, John F. Kennedy was inaugurated as the thirty-fifth president of the United States. "Let the word go forth from this time and place," he said in his inaugural address, "to friend and foe alike, that the torch has been passed to a new generation of Americans."

The new generation was eager to get a human into space. NASA planned a manned launch for March, but first, it had to run tests with living creatures. The Soviets were using dogs. NASA used primates.

On January 31, 1961, NASA sent Ham, a chimpanzee, into space. Ham was trained on a set of controls. If he wanted a banana pellet, he had to press the correct controls. If he could press the correct controls in space, then he was functioning fine in zero gravity, beyond the pull of Earth's gravity.

But Ham's mission ran into problems. His capsule was launched too high. The rocket shook too much. Just after Ham reached space, the mission was aborted, and Ham returned to Earth by his capsule parachute. He'd performed his tasks properly, however, and he was in overall good health. Maybe NASA could launch a human soon after all.

Advisers told NASA they had to send up more monkeys first. And Wernher von Braun was unhappy with those rocket vibrations. He insisted on fixing the problem. The manned launch would have to wait.

Astrochimp Ham tries out his life-support chamber prior to launch. On January 31, 1961, Ham was sent into space aboard a test Mercury capsule. His trip into space and his return helped pave the way for the manned Mercury missions.

The Huntsville Times

Man Enters Space

'So Close, Yet So Far,' Sighs Cape

U.S. Had Hoped For Own Launch

Soviet Officer Orbits Globe In 5-Ton Ship

Maximum Height Reached Reported As 188 Miles

Hobbs Admits 1944 Slaying

VON BRAUN'S REACTION:

To Keep Up, U.S.A. Must Run Like 'Hell'

Praise Is Heaped On Major Gagarin

First Man To Enter Space Is 27, Married, Father Of Two

'Worker' Stands By Story

Reds Deny Spacemen Have Died

No Astronaut Signal Received At Ft. Monmouth

Reds Win Running Lead In Race To Control Space

Today's Chuckle

Newspaper headlines announced that Russian cosmonaut Yuri Gagarin *(center)* had become the first person in space when he entered Earth's orbit aboard *Vostok 1* on April 12, 1961.

Then came the morning of April 12, 1961. John "Shorty" Powers, the spokesperson for NASA, was fast asleep when the phone rang. He answered it, barely awake.

"The Russians just put a man into space!" exclaimed a reporter. "Do you have a comment?"

Shorty was groggy. "We're all asleep down here," he grumped.

The reporter was correct. The Soviets had launched the first man into space. His name was Yuri Gagarin, and in a trip that lasted an hour and forty-eight minutes, he orbited Earth once in *Vostok 1* before parachuting back to Soviet soil.

"The first man to penetrate outer space is a Soviet man," Soviet radio broadcast to points worldwide. Thousands of Gagarin's fellow Soviets crowded into Moscow's Red Square, chanting his name.

The White House complimented the Soviets on their accomplishment but through gritted teeth. President Kennedy called a meeting of his space advisers. He was impatient. "Is there any place we can catch them? What can we do? Can we go around the Moon before them?" Maybe, said his advisers, but it would take a lot more money. And this was no time for mistakes.

"If somebody can just tell me how to catch up," said the president. "I don't care if it's the janitor over there, if he knows how." Then he looked at each man carefully and said, "There's nothing more important."

Soon after, Kennedy faced worse news. Since Eisenhower's presidency, the United States had been secretly training a group of Cubans who lived in the United States to overthrow Castro in Cuba. But when these refugee soldiers invaded Cuba's Bay of Pigs, it was a total disaster. Between Gagarin and the Bay of Pigs, President Kennedy was beginning to look downright ineffective against the country's Cold War enemies.

"He Is A-OK"

On the morning of May 5, 1961, astronaut Alan Shepard, wearing a silver space suit, eased into a tiny capsule atop a Redstone rocket. Nobody was insisting on putting more monkeys into space, not after Gagarin's voyage. It was time to send up an American.

The launch was scheduled for 7:20 A.M., but there was one delay after another. Strapped into *Freedom 7*, as he'd named his capsule, Shepard eventually had to go to the bathroom. But the flight was supposed to be so short that no provisions had been made for such a need. Finally, Shepard couldn't stand it any longer. He simply urinated in his suit.

What was taking so long anyhow? Forty-five million people watching on television must have wondered the same thing. The Russians had shot their man into space nearly a month ago! In *Freedom 7*,

Shepard radioed Mission Control asking, "Why don't you fellows solve your little problem and light this candle?"

On the freeways in Los Angeles, California, traffic slowed as people listened to the launch countdown on their car radios. Taxi drivers in Manhattan (New York) ignored people hailing them so they could hear every word. And in Washington, D.C., President Kennedy watched "with his hands jammed in his pockets," said Hugh Sidey, White House correspondent for *Time* magazine, "expecting the worst."

Just after 9:30 A.M., according to *Time,* a man ran out of a barbershop in New Jersey. "He's up!" he yelled. Alan Shepard was in space.

"The astronaut reports that he is A-OK," NASA spokesperson Shorty Powers happily told the press. Shepard hadn't used that exact term, but Powers used it so often while millions of people were tuned

Alan Shepard, the first U.S. astronaut in space, adjusts his helmet moments before reentering Earth's atmosphere on May 5, 1961.

in that "A-OK" became a common term. By the time Shepard splashed down in the Atlantic Ocean fifteen minutes later, he was a national hero.

His feat gave the country—and President Kennedy—a great, welcome boost of confidence. Less than three weeks later, Kennedy addressed Congress: "I believe that this nation should commit itself to achieving the goal, before this decade is out, of landing a man on the Moon and returning him safely to Earth."

"My heart almost stopped," remembered Christopher Kraft, NASA's first flight director. "Did he say what I thought I heard?" According to the space advisers, the United States would be able to achieve the goal, given proper funding and dedicated human resources.

On July 21, 1961, Gus Grissom was launched into space in his capsule, the *Liberty Bell*. That made it two Americans in space versus just one Soviet!

But the Soviets had plans of their own. On August 6, 1961, they launched cosmonaut Gherman Titov into space. He orbited Earth seventeen times in his capsule, *Vostok 2*. The Americans had never orbited Earth. The Soviets had one-upped the United States again.

A week later, the Soviets began building the Berlin Wall. The city of Berlin, Germany, was a most unusual city. After World War II, it had been divided into West Berlin, part of democratic West Germany, and East Berlin, which, like East Germany, was under Communist control. The people of East Berlin attempted to escape to West Berlin so frequently that the Soviets answered by erecting the massive Berlin Wall between the two parts of the city. In Berlin the Iron Curtain was real. It was made of brick topped with barbed wire.

John Glenn, "The Bravest Man"

For months there were no manned launches in either the United States or the Soviet Union. Then came February 20, 1962. That day,

John Glenn steps into his Mercury capsule, *Friendship 7*, atop an Atlas rocket on February 20, 1962. Glenn made history that day, becoming the first U.S. astronaut to orbit Earth.

astronaut John Glenn became the first American to orbit Earth. He circled the planet three times in a trip that took just under five hours. From his spacecraft, *Friendship 7*, he saw lights from cities below, dust storms crossing Africa, and three sunsets. When the automatic system malfunctioned, Glenn became the first person in space— American or Soviet—to pilot a spacecraft using its hand controls. The trip back to Earth was the biggest challenge. Because of an equipment problem, Glenn was forced to steer *Friendship 7* through a fiery, bumpy descent into Earth's atmosphere. Thanks to his skill and courage, he splashed down safely in the Atlantic Ocean.

One hundred million people watched Glenn's flight. So many people crowded into Cocoa Beach, Florida, to watch the launch that it took many of them longer to get back to the main road than it took Glenn to circle Earth. Most people, however, watched on television or listened on the radio.

A high school boy wrote to Glenn that he "rolled out of bed at 4:00 A.M. to watch. I sat spellbound in front of the T.V. I skipped school so I could watch your flight. So did a couple of my buddies. You're pretty popular with us but the Principal was beginning to have his doubts."

Glenn was hailed as a national hero. "You are the bravest man I ever saw," a third-grade boy wrote to Glenn. Citizens named streets and schools after him. Parents named their newborns after him. One boy even named his hamster John H. Glenn. "The H. is for hamster," he said.

Not everyone was jubilant about Glenn's flight, however. P. L. Prattis, an African American, wrote in the *New Pittsburgh Courier*, "If seven men had been needed to clean out the space capsule Glenn rode in then they would have thought of me and six others like me." He added, "I'm tired of wielding mops. I want to go to the Moon."

Nevertheless, the enthusiasm for Glenn and his mission was so high worldwide that NASA sent his space capsule, *Friendship 7*, on a tour of seventeen countries. Millions of people came to see it. The capsule then made a stop at the Seattle World's Fair, which had opened in Washington in April 1962. The fair's theme was "Man in the Space Age," and its most recognizable symbol was a huge tower called the Space Needle. The U.S. Spacearium exhibit featured a simulated ride in a spaceship.

Inside *Friendship 7*, Glenn is in a state of weightlessness—traveling at 17,500 miles per hour (28,163 km per hour)—during an orbit of Earth. Glenn made three orbits before reentering Earth's atmosphere and returning home a national hero.

The Russian cosmonaut Gherman Titov, touring the United States, also appeared at the World's Fair. Throughout his trip, he boasted about Soviet superiority. John Glenn wanted to show him a bit of the real United States, and invited him and his wife, Tamara, to his house near Washington, D.C., for a cookout. When Titov and his entourage arrived, Glenn was in his carport frantically trying to put out a grill fire. "The steaks survived the disaster and were delicious," Glenn remembered. "Titov later told me that evening was the most fun he and Tamara had had in Washington."

The End of Mercury

Astronaut Scott Carpenter was the next American in space. On May 24, 1962, he orbited Earth three times. The Soviets hadn't sent a person into space since Titov, but the first anniversary of the formidable Berlin Wall was coming up, and Premier Khrushchev wanted to celebrate it on a grand scale. In August 1962, the Soviets launched two spacecraft, *Vostok 3* and *Vostok 4*. They eventually came within 3 miles (5 km) of each other. The two cosmonauts, Andrian Nikolayev and Pavel Popovitch, even sang duets with each other.

The "rendezvous," as the *New York Times* called it, was "a spectacular accomplishment." Except it wasn't a rendezvous at all. A real rendezvous would have required the capsules to be equipped with guidance technology that would have enabled the cosmonauts to steer their crafts closer to each other. The Soviet capsules had simply used the physics of orbits and well-timed launches to whiz within a few miles of each other at more than 5,000 miles (8,047 km) an hour. But the Soviets saw no need to correct the world. If everyone wanted to believe it was a rendezvous, then very well. The mission was "one more vivid proof of the superiority of [Communism] over capitalism," said cosmonaut Nikolayev.

The United States seemed to be back in the same old number two position in the race for space. To bolster confidence in the space pro-

Technicians and flight controllers man their stations at the Manned Spacecraft Center in Houston, Texas, during the 1960s. Astronauts and mission staff called the center Mission Control or simply Houston.

gram, President Kennedy toured the country's space facilities, including Cape Canaveral in Florida and the Marshall Space Flight Center (formerly the Redstone Arsenal) in Huntsville, Alabama. His final stop was a new complex outside of Houston, Texas, called the Manned Spacecraft Center. The center would be home to NASA's new mission control center and engineering and testing facilities.

In Houston President Kennedy spoke before a huge crowd at the Rice University football stadium. "This generation does not intend to founder in the backwash of the coming age of space," he said with conviction. "We mean to be a part of it, we mean to lead it."

At the Manned Spacecraft Center, he met with top staff about NASA's plans. They showed him the designs for the spacecraft to be used someday for manned lunar voyages. The designs included a command service module, which would orbit the Moon, and a lunar module, which would take astronauts to the Moon's surface.

"I'll be following your progress," the president told them, "and I'm looking forward to that lunar landing."

Soon NASA named nine new astronauts. Then in October 1962, astronaut Wally Schirra orbited Earth six times in a perfect mission.

Soon after, however, the United States came face-to-face with the grimmest sort of Cold War news. The Soviets, it was learned, were getting ready to deploy nuclear missiles in Cuba, missiles that would be aimed at the United States. President Kennedy ordered U.S. ships to blockade Cuba to prevent any ships from entering Cuba's waters.

This aerial image shows Soviet-made missiles, transporters, and launchers in Cuba in October 1962. The missiles led to the Cuban Missile Crisis—a time of dangerously tense relations between the United States and the Soviet Union.

Steve Jobs, cofounder of Apple Computer, was seven years old then. "I probably didn't sleep for three or four nights because I was afraid that if I went to sleep, I wouldn't wake up." People all over the United States were worried about an attack from Cuban missiles.

After thirteen tense days, Kennedy reached an agreement with Khrushchev. Among other terms, the United States would agree to never invade Cuba if the Soviets would turn their ships around and remove their missiles from Cuba. The crisis was over.

On May 15, 1963, NASA prepared to launch astronaut Gordon Cooper into space. While awaiting liftoff, Cooper not only wasn't nervous, he *fell asleep*! But he woke up for the launch and orbited Earth twenty-two times in *Faith 7*.

The goals of Project Mercury had been achieved. It was time for NASA to move on to the Gemini program.

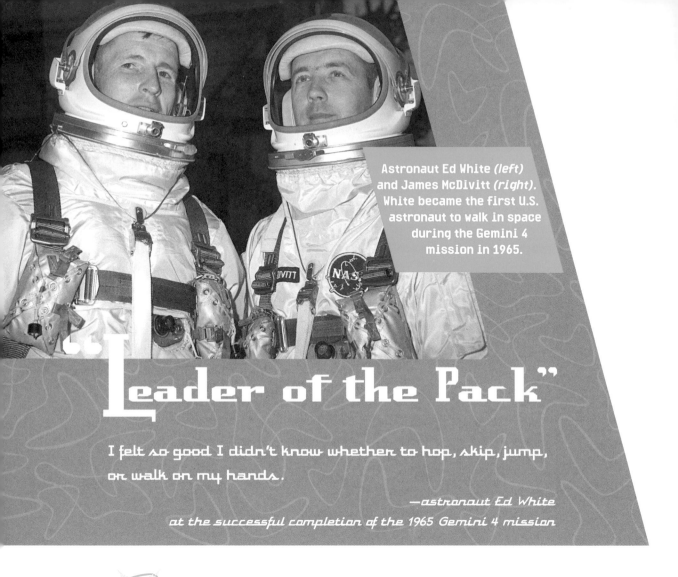

"Leader of the Pack"

I felt so good I didn't know whether to hop, skip, jump, or walk on my hands.

—astronaut Ed White at the successful completion of the 1965 Gemini 4 mission

The early sixties in the United States was a time of great optimism. Anything, it seemed, was possible. Any problem could be solved with the right mix of dedication and brainpower. The future looked bright, and a sense of possibility inspired people in all walks of life.

It wouldn't be long, it appeared, before the world looked just as it did on *The Jetsons*. *The Jetsons*, an animated comedy, debuted on American TV in September 1962. It featured George Jetson and his family in the year 2062. They lived in the Sky Pad Apartments, an ultra-high-rise building on a pole. George flew to work in a little bubblelike car that he could fold up into a suitcase when he reached the office. The family maid was a robot, and Jane, George's wife, cooked mostly by pressing buttons.

One regular viewer remembers, "I liked the way George zipped around in that space car. Everything on the show," he said, looked "very modern. I liked it."

In fact, the Jetsons' modern look was popular in the United States of the early sixties, as well. Trendsetting furniture designers embraced the shapes of the space race. The sphere—the shape of *Sputnik* and other satellites, as well as the Moon—inspired new creations such as designer Eero Aarnio's Ball Chair. The Ball Chair, made of fiberglass,

A still (image) from *The Jetsons*—a space-age animated cartoon that first aired in the United States in 1962. The program further popularized the space age with TV viewers.

looked like a personal space capsule. Verner Panton's Moon Lamp, a series of nested aluminum hoops, was another example of the look. Aarnio and Panton, like many designers of the era, adopted not just the shapes of the space age but also its lightweight materials, developing furniture from plastic, wire, and foam. The sleek, lightweight designs reflected the new sense of mobility people felt. Spaceship colors such as chrome, white, and clear were popular too. The inflatable *Echo* satellite inspired the lightest furniture of all: inflatable chairs.

Barbara D'Arcy White, a furniture room designer at Bloomingdale's in New York City, remembers, "We were the first department store ever to have a chrome-and-glass cocktail table." The design, she notes, "was very radical. People were hungry for that stuff."

Architects embraced a futuristic look as well. In the early 1960s, the TWA Terminal at Idlewild Airport (later renamed John F. Kennedy Airport) opened outside of New York City. Designed by Eero Saarinen, a famous Finnish architect, the terminal with its wing-like roof looked as if it could take flight at any moment.

Then there was Anaheim, California. It looked as much like George Jetson's hometown as nearly any place in the country. There was Satellite Shopland mall, with its huge, rotating sphere. The Anaheim Convention Center looked like one big flying saucer. Out-of-towners visiting Disneyland, Anaheim's main attraction, could bunk in at the Astro Motel, the Cosmic Lodge Inn, or the Inn of Tomorrow. The buildings' designs, which included lots of glass, steel, and neon, reflected "the excitement and enthusiasm of the era," said John English, an architectural preservationist.

Woman in Space

American enthusiasm took a hit on June 16, 1963, though, when the Soviets made another of their groundbreaking announcements. Not only had they again launched two spacecraft, *Vostok 5* and *Vostok 6*, but *Vostok 6* was "manned" by *a woman*! Valentina Tereshkova orbited Earth forty-eight times. According to Premier Khrushchev, Tereshkova's mission was proof of "the equality of men and women in our country."

American Jane Hart responded, "I'm more annoyed at the fact than I am impressed . . . the U.S. is a hundred years behind in using the full abilities of women."

In June 1963, the Soviets bested the United States once again when they put the first woman, Valentina Tereshkova, in space. Cosmonaut Tereshkova—broadcasting live from her space capsule at right—orbited Earth forty-eight times.

Hart spoke from experience. In 1961 she had brought home three carts full of groceries, stocked her freezer, and made sure her husband and eight children would have regular milk deliveries. She had then flown to Albuquerque, New Mexico, one of a select group of thirteen experienced women pilots to undergo astronaut testing. The Lovelace Foundation, which had tested the Mercury Seven astronauts, put the women through the same rigorous experiments as it had the men. Women tended to be smaller than men, and they used less oxygen. They'd be well suited for traveling in tiny space capsules. The Mercury Thirteen, as the women were later called, scored well on the tests. Yet NASA refused to accept them as astronauts, citing that it did not "have a requirement for such a program."

Women were making quiet headway in the space program, however, as engineers, chemists, mathematicians, astronomers, and more. Edith Olson, a chemist, helped create the first electronic circuits. "It's like printing all the works in the Library of Congress on a grain of rice," she said, but instead of words and books, the tiny circuits held electrical components. Bea Finkelstein, a nutritionist, developed space food. The astronauts referred to her lab as Bea's Diner. Engineer Joan Fencl Bowski helped design the Mercury space capsule at McDonnell Aircraft in Saint Louis, Missouri. Prior to Alan Shepard's launch, she requested a transfer to Cape Canaveral. She wanted to be there when Shepard went up in the McDonnell capsule. But McDonnell refused the transfer because there were no women's bathroom facilities there.

When Grown-Ups Cried

In October 1963, President Kennedy presented the Collier Trophy, a prestigious aviation award, to the Mercury Seven astronauts "as a stimulus to astronauts who will carry our flag to the Moon—and perhaps, some day, beyond."

The following month, President Kennedy made a trip to Texas. On November 22, he was riding in a parade through Dallas, Texas, in an

President John F. Kennedy *(center)* reels to his left after being struck by a sniper's bullet in Dallas, Texas, on November 22, 1963. The assassination of John F. Kennedy shocked the nation and the world.

open convertible. Suddenly, there was the sound of gunfire. An assassin had shot the president.

The news spread quickly as reporters interrupted television soap operas and radio programs with special bulletins. People hurried to churches to pray. Teachers struggled to keep teaching.

Less than an hour later, in New York City, "the great bells of St. Patrick's Cathedral began to toll solemnly," reported the *New York Times*. "The crowd passing on Fifth Avenue looked up and knew." President Kennedy was dead.

For many kids, it was the first time they'd seen their parents cry. For days virtually nothing was on television but coverage of the assassination and the funeral.

Vice President Lyndon B. Johnson was sworn in as the thirty-sixth president. Under Johnson, the space program was in good hands.

From the time of the *Sputnik 1* launch in 1957, Johnson had recognized the potential of space exploration. As Senate majority leader, he had initiated congressional hearings to determine why the Russians had been first in space. Johnson had helped to develop the Space Act that created NASA and had seen to it that Congress passed the legislation.

New York World's Fair

In April 1964, optimism found a new home at the New York World's Fair. The Seattle World's Fair had had the Space Needle. In New York, the signature structure was the Unisphere, a twelve-story-high model of Earth encircled by the orbit tracks of three satellites.

For many participants, the fair was an opportunity to look ahead to a dazzling future in which technology would solve the world's problems. General Motors' Futurama exhibit offered models of cities of the future, including an underwater city and a city in space. The Du Pont pavilion staged a musical with songs such as "The Happy Plastic Family." The IBM Company introduced the Selectric, the Typewriter of the Future, by topping its pavilion with an oversized model of the Selectric's typewriter ball. (Little did they know that computers would soon make typewriters seem old-fashioned.) Another company exhibited a dishwasher that took dirty plastic plates, ground them up, then made brand new plates from them.

The fair embraced the space age in its architecture as well. The New York Port Authority pavilion, for instance, resembled a spaceship perched atop a huge stand.

Fairgoers who wanted to see real spacecraft could visit the 2-acre (0.8-hectare) U.S. Space Park. Exhibits included the *Aurora 7*, in which Scott Carpenter had orbited Earth, the *Explorer 1* (the first U.S. satellite), and an Atlas rocket. The fair also featured a lunar module and a stage, or section, of a Saturn V rocket, to be used for a Moon launch. Nearby stood a Titan II rocket and a two-person

The space age was the main theme of the 1964 World's Fair in New York City. The theme is evident in the fair's structures, including the Unisphere *(center, with criss-cross orbit paths)*, and surrounding buildings.

spacecraft. This equipment was for Project Gemini, NASA's current program, which involved some of the agency's most exciting work.

The Gemini Program

The Gemini program had three goals, all part of the long-range goal of landing a person on the Moon. During Gemini, NASA would launch two-person missions of increasing duration, achieve the ability to control the movements of its spacecraft, and master the skill of docking two spacecraft in space.

Gemini astronauts would require an array of skills and survival techniques. They trained fifty hours a week for two to five years to prepare for one mission. They spent long hours in simulators, which reproduced what it would be like in the spacecraft, learning how to pilot it. But that was just the start. If they unexpectedly needed to eject from their capsules, they would have to know how to survive in any climate or place. They learned how to catch, skin, and cook iguanas, and they sampled a spit-roasted boa constrictor. "It tasted like a four-foot long [1.3-meter] hot dog," said one astronaut. They learned how to make clothes from parachutes. They also studied geology and astronomy in order to make informed observations on their missions.

Meanwhile, NASA and its contractors, the companies it hired, were working to solve a host of problems. For instance, they needed to find a way to keep track of the millions of parts used to build the various spacecraft. The solution they developed is a familiar part of modern daily life: bar codes.

A Great Society

In 1964, a presidential election year, President Lyndon B. Johnson won the office by a landslide. LBJ, as he was known, had big plans for the United States. He envisioned what he called a Great Society in which poverty would be eliminated. Federal programs would help to end hunger and improve housing and education.

But there were other demands on President Johnson's agenda. One was the Vietnam War (1957–1975) in Southeast Asia. The Vietnam War was complicated. Simply put, the United States had become involved in this conflict as a result of the Cold War. U.S. troops were sent to aid the South Vietnamese to prevent a takeover by the Communist North Vietnamese. The trouble was the South Vietnamese were divided over the direction their country should go. Nonetheless, by July 1965, President Johnson had sent more than one hundred thousand U.S. troops to Vietnam.

Martin Luther King Jr. *(fourth from left)* joins peaceful demonstrators during the 1963 March on Washington. At the event, King delivered his "I have a dream" speech, calling for civil rights and equality for all Americans.

President Johnson also pushed for the passage of a sweeping civil rights bill that President Kennedy had introduced. The previous August, the Reverend Martin Luther King Jr. had stood at the top of the steps of the Lincoln Memorial, before almost a quarter of a million people who had gathered for the March on Washington. "I have a dream," he said. "I have a dream that my four little children will one day live in a nation where they will not be judged by the color of their skin but by the content of their character." The speech, which was broadcast on television, helped build support for the civil rights movement.

Within the next year, Congress had passed the Voting Rights Act, to ensure every citizen, regardless of race, would be allowed to vote, and the Civil Rights Act, to make discrimination unlawful. But not all whites embraced the changes in the law. Southern blacks who registered to vote were often threatened and beaten. Activists poured into the South to try to help forward their cause. One of them was Alvin J. Bronstein, a civil rights lawyer from New York. He and his colleagues had no time for the space race.

"In those days, the civil rights movement and activity was so intense that there was no time for anything else," he remembered. "Folks lived, breathed and almost exclusively talked about 'the movement.'"

Gemini Milestones

Meanwhile, the folks at NASA were living and breathing the space program. The Soviets "had the advantage of knowing exactly what we were going to do, and when," said Chris Kraft, "simply by reading the newspapers." The Soviets, who kept their plans secret, knew that NASA was planning a two-person Gemini launch. So what did they do? On October 12, 1964, they launched three men into space in *Voskhod 1*. To the world, the Soviets appeared to have made a technological leap by designing a spacecraft for three. All they'd really done, it was learned years later, was strip down an old Vostok spacecraft until it could accommodate three cosmonauts. The men were so squeezed for space that they had no room for bulky space suits. So they went without, despite the risk involved. If anything happened to the spacecraft, the three suitless cosmonauts had no chance of surviving in outer space. The world saw none of the shortcuts, though. It simply saw that the Soviets had launched three men into space before the United States had even launched two.

But the Soviets weren't done! In March 1965, they sent up *Voskhod 2*, with two cosmonauts. One of them, Alexei Leonov, crawled out of the capsule's air lock and walked in space. Thanks to a camera, amazing images of his walk were sent back to Earth.

What didn't end up on film was the trouble Leonov faced upon his return to the capsule. His space suit became so superinflated that he couldn't fit back through the air lock. He had to release oxygen from his suit, a bit at a time, to get back in.

Five days later, the United States launched *Gemini 3*, its first two-man mission. Astronauts John Young and Gus Grissom would test how well they could maneuver the spacecraft. Without maneuverability, there could be no docking, or linking, of spacecraft, which would be essential to a Moon landing.

They'd also be sampling freeze-dried space food, which the astronauts didn't find appetizing. So before they were sealed into their capsule, Wally Schirra slipped a package to John Young. While Gus Grissom fumbled with his freeze-dried meal, Young unwrapped the package an honest-to-goodness corned beef sandwich from Wolfie's Deli in Cocoa Beach. But it had honest-to-goodness crumbs too that floated all over in zero gravity. Those crumbs could have destroyed expensive equipment, so they quickly rewrapped the sandwich.

Angry congressional leaders attacked NASA for the incident. A NASA administrator finally assured them that the agency would "prevent the occurrence of corned beef sandwiches in future flights."

Sandwich aside, the *Gemini 3* mission was a success. "Gemini's a Corvette [a sports car]," said Grissom. The astronauts could easily maneuver it in any direction. The Soviets had no such capability. But the ability to maneuver their spacecraft "looked puny to politicians, and even to some reporters, when compared to what the Russians had done with Alexei Leonov's space walk," noted Chris Kraft.

NASA silenced its critics on June 3, 1965. The mission at hand was *Gemini 4*, with astronauts Ed White and Jim McDivitt. That day Ed White became the first American to perform an extravehicular activity (EVA), or space walk.

For twenty minutes, White had a grand time floating around in space, attached to the capsule by only a cable. He was able to control his movements with a handheld maneuvering unit. Cosmonaut Alexei Leonov had been able only to drift. White had such a good time that he called his return to the vehicle "the saddest moment of my life."

Astronaut Ed White floats weightless above Earth on June 3, 1965, during the first space walk taken by a U.S. astronaut. His success silenced critics, who believed the United States couldn't compete with the Soviet Union.

"Ed's space walk completely eclipsed the Russians," noted Chris Kraft. The *Gemini 4* mission was also the first time NASA used the new mission control center at Houston's Manned Spacecraft Center. This time, Nikita Khrushchev had no clever response. Leonid Brezhnev had succeeded him as the Soviet premier.

"Space, the Final Frontier"

Space was a popular theme on television shows of this era. *Lost in Space*, which premiered in September 1965, told the story of the Robinsons, an American family who became lost in space en route to colonizing another planet. A stowaway, the evil and cowardly Dr. Smith, caused trouble in every adventure-filled episode. There were encounters with a carnivorous Cyclops, a robot with a will of its own, aliens who planned to steal the Robinsons' brains! The show was supposed to take place in the distant year of . . . 1997!

Then there was *I Dream of Jeannie*. This weekly sitcom was pure fun. When astronaut Major Tony Nelson's space capsule splashed down near a deserted island, he discovered a bottle containing a genie. Jeannie, as the good-hearted but meddlesome genie was named, proceeded to wreak disorder in his orderly astronaut life. "Oh, Master!" she exclaimed each time she ruined yet another Moon mission or training exercise.

In 1966 a new science fiction show called *Star Trek* made its debut. *Star Trek*, which took place in the far-off future, followed the crew of the starship *Enterprise* into "Space: the final frontier . . . its five year mission to . . . boldly go where no man has gone before." Captain James T. Kirk, played by William Shatner, commanded the *Enterprise,* assisted by Lieutenant Commander Spock, a pointy-eared Vulcan played by Leonard Nimoy. The *Enterprise* crew (which looked to many viewers as if they were wearing their pajamas) patrolled space, said Shatner in an interview, "in the same way the Navy vessels in the eighteenth century patrolled the outer reaches of the Empire."

Star Trek ultimately became such a cultural fixture that people who had never watched the show were known to quote lines from it, like, "It's life, Jim, but not as we know it." And "Beam me up, Scotty!" was a way of saying, "Get me out of here!"

(From left to right) Captain James T. Kirk (William Shatner), Dr. Leonard McCoy (DeForest Kelley), and First Officer Spock (Leonard Nimoy) of the hit show *Star Trek*

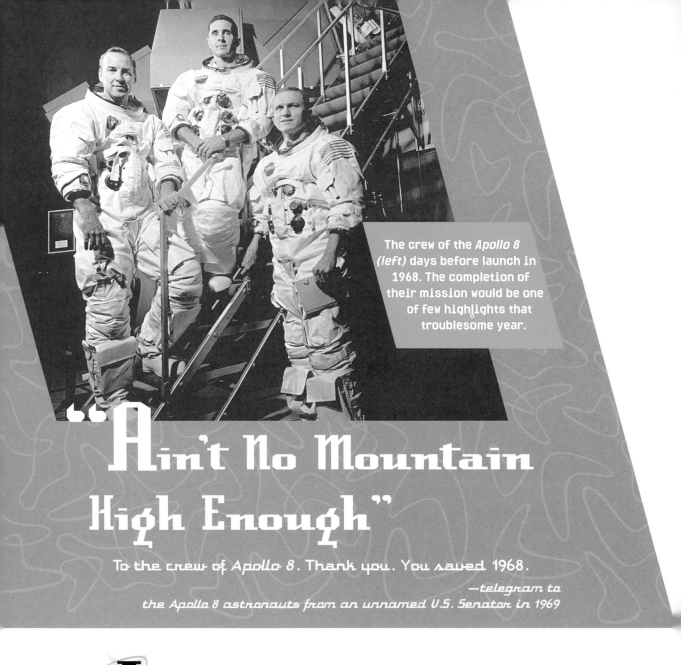

The crew of the *Apollo 8* *(left)* days before launch in 1968. The completion of their mission would be one of few highlights that troublesome year.

"Ain't No Mountain High Enough"

To the crew of *Apollo 8*. Thank you. You saved 1968.

—telegram to
the Apollo 8 astronauts from an unnamed U.S. Senator in 1969

In Ridgefield, Connecticut, a seven-year-old boy named Mark Salzman decided to become an astronaut. "I didn't mean when I grew up," he said. "I meant right then, preferably by the end of the month." He wrote to NASA and was sent an envelope full of pamphlets.

"One of the pamphlets showed an astronaut tucked inside a cramped mock capsule," he remembered. The pamphlet explained that "the astronauts had to get used to spending many long hours without being able to move." So Salzman set out to set a record for "sitting still in a cramped space" to impress the folks at NASA.

"I found a cardboard box I could barely fit into," he explained, "drew buttons and gauges all over the inside of it and outfitted it with a blanket, a thermometer, an alarm clock and a periscope made with two of my mother's compact mirrors." Every day he sat in the box for a longer and longer time. By the time he could last over an hour, he was getting bored. So he "started pointing the box toward the TV so I could watch my favorite program—*Lost in Space*—through the periscope."

He'd worked his way up to a three-hour stay when, one afternoon, he heard a pop! The box was coming apart!

His mother was in the room teaching a piano lesson. "My butt had popped out of the spaceship," remembered Salzman, "right in front of one of Mom's teen-age piano students." So ended his career as an astronaut. (He became a writer and tells this story in his book, *Lost in Place*.)

The astronauts at NASA had better luck with their long-term missions. Gordon Cooper and Pete Conrad of the *Gemini 5* mission spent eight days in their capsule in August 1965. Even the Soviets couldn't match that record. Then, in December 1965, astronauts Jim Lovell and Frank Borman, aboard their *Gemini 7* spacecraft, stayed in space for fourteen days. "Imagine spending two weeks in a men's room," said Lovell. More important, during their mission, they were able to rendezvous in space with another spacecraft, the *Gemini 6*, manned by astronauts Wally Schirra and Tom Stafford. They maneuvered the two spacecraft to within 1 foot (0.3 m) of each other. "America could now officially claim to be ahead of the Russians in the race to the Moon," noted Chris Kraft.

The *Gemini 6* and *7* missions ended with the first live televised splashdowns ever. In just nine months, from March to December

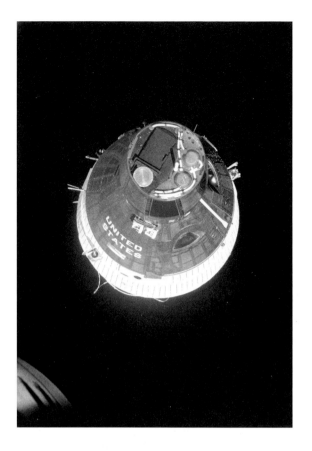

This photograph shows *Gemini 7* viewed through the hatch window of *Gemini 6* in December 1965. The astronauts maneuvered their capsules to within 1 foot (0.3 m) of each other.

1965, NASA had sent up five Gemini spacecraft and ten astronauts, performed a space walk, and completed a rendezvous. The Soviets, on the other hand, hadn't sent anyone into space since Leonov made his space walk back in March of that year.

As the Gemini program moved swiftly along, the growing space industry was pumping money and jobs into the economy. An old hosiery mill in Massachusetts became the production plant for guidance instruments. On the Gulf Coast of Mississippi, a swampy stretch of land was being turned into a rocket-testing ground. Construction crews relocated graves in the area so the rockets' vibrations wouldn't destroy the headstones. The new NASA project in Mississippi was expected to employ as many as eleven thousand people, usually at pay scales higher than what was typical in the region. It was drawing new businesses such as motels and stores. More than one million dollars was going toward improving telephone, electrical, and gas services in the area. Hundreds of new homes were under construction. The same scenario was being repeated in booming new aerospace communities across the country.

The End of Gemini

In March 1966, *Gemini 8* astronauts Neil Armstrong and Dave Scott docked their capsule with an unmanned spacecraft that had been launched separately. It was the first successful docking in space. On the trip back, however, the astronauts ran into trouble. Their rocket thrusters refused to turn off. The spacecraft started to roll, pitching the men around the craft. "We have a serious problem here," Scott radioed back.

The television networks broke into their regular programming to follow the crisis. One update interrupted *Lost in Space*. Some viewers

Gemini 8 astronauts Neil Armstrong and Dave Scott pilot their capsule toward an unmanned spacecraft *(above)*. The men completed the first successful docking in space in March 1966.

were so incensed by the interruption that they complained to the network. They were more interested in pretend space than a real space crisis! Armstrong and Scott, staying calm throughout, solved the problem and landed safely.

In the four remaining Gemini missions, astronauts fine-tuned rendezvous and docking techniques. When *Gemini 12* astronauts Jim Lovell and Buzz Aldrin walked out to the launchpad for the last Gemini mission in November 1966, they wore signs on their backs: Lovell's read, "The," and Aldrin's read, "End." It was time to move on to the Apollo program and, in the words of *Star Trek*, "boldly go where no man has gone before." It was time to head for the Moon.

"Get Us Out!"

The main goal of the Apollo program was to land Americans on the Moon and return them safely to Earth. NASA also planned to explore the Moon for scientific purposes and develop the ability of humans to function there.

After the success of the Gemini program, most Americans felt optimistic about the space program. What's more, the Soviet Union hadn't launched a man into space since 1965. The United States was winning the space race!

Then in early 1967, three astronauts—Gus Grissom, Roger Chaffee, and Ed White—were training for the first Apollo mission. Grissom, one of the original Mercury Seven astronauts, had been the second American in space. White was the astronaut who had so enjoyed his space walk, the first by an American, that he hadn't wanted to return to the capsule. Chaffee was newer to NASA and had yet to go into space.

On January 27, they were conducting a simulation exercise in their capsule. The pressurized atmosphere in the craft was pure oxygen. When a spark burst from an exposed wire, it flared immediately into a blazing fire.

The scorched *Apollo 1* capsule awaits investigation by NASA technicians following a devastating fire that killed three U.S. astronauts in 1967.

"Fire in the spacecraft!" yelled one of the astronauts. "Get us out!" But the hatch was not designed to pop open. In eighteen seconds, all three men were dead.

A review team spent months picking through the charred remains to identify the cause of the fire. The use of pure oxygen had been a dangerous choice, and the hatch was too difficult to open. The team also found evidence of shoddy workmanship.

NASA set out to shape up its operation. It implemented list after list of improvements, including a hatch that could be opened in ten seconds, nonflammable components, and a replacement of the pure oxygen with a nitrogen and oxygen mix.

That April the Soviet space program suffered a tragedy as well. Soviet cosmonaut Vladimir Komarov was killed during the Soviets' first manned mission in two years. Komarov was returning to Earth aboard *Soyuz 1*, the Soviets' newest spacecraft, when the vehicle's parachutes malfunctioned and it crashed.

That October marked ten years since the Soviets had launched *Sputnik 1*. During that time, the race for space had focused on manned space missions. However, both countries also had been busy launching probes, or unmanned spacecraft. In early 1966, the Soviets were the first to soft-land a probe, *Luna 9*, on the Moon. NASA successfully landed *Surveyor 1* on the lunar surface several months later. The probes sent back photographs and other information. In 1967 both countries had succeeded in sending probes past Venus.

Still, in the wake of the *Apollo 1* disaster, the U.S. space program seemed to have come to a standstill. It roared back to life in November 1967. That month NASA launched an unmanned Saturn V rocket, the rocket that would hurl an Apollo spacecraft toward the Moon. Thirty stories tall, the Saturn V was an "impressive monster," said Chris Kraft. At the time of liftoff, CBS news anchor Walter Cronkite was 3 miles (5 km) away in press headquarters. Even from that distance, he said, "the building shook, acoustical tiles in our ceiling bounced out of their frames, soft drink bottles walked off the desk, and [the] window vibrated and bulged." The Saturn V did its job: it launched an unmanned Apollo spacecraft more than 11,000 miles (17,700 km) into space.

Major Matt Mason and Friends

For kids who yearned to launch their own Saturn V, Sears offered a three-stage rocket, 20 inches (51 cm) high, that could launch a capsule 10 feet (3 m) in the air. "It's like being at Cape Kennedy when the countdown begins," said the catalog. If that didn't excite kids, Sears also offered the Billy Blastoff set; a Johnny Astro Launching Station; and Moon McDare, an action figure, and his faithful pal, Space Mutt.

Space toys had been around since long before *Sputnik,* but the selection had been small. By the mid-1960s, at the height of the space race, toy companies offered junior astronauts a wealth of choices. *Lost in Space* fans could buy toy versions of the *Lost in Space* robot and the *Lost in Space* ray gun. In 1967 a new astronaut appeared. He was Major Matt Mason, Mattel's Man in Space, and he stood 6 inches (15 cm) tall.

"My mom didn't allow army toys," remembered one fan. "But I could have Major Mason dolls because they were explorers, not fighters. . . . I had just about every accessory." That meant the Moon Crawler, the Space Station, the talking jet pack, and more.

Ironically, the Barbie doll was ahead of them all. Although NASA's Apollo program had no female astronauts, Mattel had introduced Barbie the Astronaut in 1965.

1968

The United States had come a long way since that night in October 1957 when *Sputnik 1* first had passed overhead. Now the innocence of *Leave It to Beaver* seemed to be part of the past, replaced by more turbulent times.

As 1968 began, approximately half a million Americans were serving in Vietnam. As the number of deaths increased, the antiwar movement had grown as well. Young men resisted being drafted or forced into military service. "Hell no, we won't go!" students protested on college campuses across the country. Demonstrators marched on Washington, and young men burned their draft cards.

Through it all, the nation's military leaders maintained that the United States was winning the war. But in late January, during the holiday called Tet, the North Vietnamese launched a huge attack on more than thirty-five South Vietnamese cities and towns. The Tet offensive resulted in massive death and destruction. Footage of the fighting appeared on the news back home, and more Americans than ever began to question the war.

It was another presidential election year. President Lyndon B. Johnson had hoped to build a Great Society. But the demands of the Vietnam War had outpaced his plans for changes at home. The president's approval rating had sunk to 40 percent. In the meantime, Democratic candidate Senator Eugene McCarthy of Minnesota was attracting voters with his antiwar message. Johnson realized there was no way he was going to win another term as president. On March 31, he announced he would not run for reelection.

Just days later, on April 4, the Reverend Martin Luther King Jr. was assassinated in Memphis, Tennessee. The civil rights movement had lost its brightest beacon. Angry riots erupted in cities across the country.

But the killing wasn't over. Senator Robert Kennedy of New York, brother of President John F. Kennedy, had also entered the presidential race as an antiwar candidate. On June 4, 1968, he too was assassinated.

Civil rights leader Martin Luther King Jr. lies fatally wounded from an assassin's bullet outside his hotel room in Memphis, Tennessee, on April 4, 1968. The year was marred by violence and great social unrest.

By the time the Democratic Convention was held that summer in Chicago, Illinois, the bad feelings that had been festering all year were stronger than ever. The Democrats were on the verge of nominating Vice President Hubert Humphrey of Minnesota, who supported the war, as their candidate. Ten thousand young protesters went to Chicago to demonstrate against Humphrey and against the war. But Chicago mayor Richard J. Daley wasn't about to let a bunch of rabble-rousing kids get the upper hand in his city. He ordered twenty-three thousand police and members of the National Guard to the scene. By the time the convention ended, the police had brutalized not only the demonstrators but also bystanders, including children, clubbing them, beating them, and attacking them with tear gas. The violence was caught on camera for the world to see.

The news in 1968 had been one awful thing after another. "Thank God I've still got my astronauts," said President Johnson.

Space Odyssey

The summer of 1968 brought a most unusual space movie to theaters. It featured no killer Martians nor invading aliens. Instead, Stanley Kubrick's *2001: A Space Odyssey*, based on a book by Arthur C. Clarke, included apes, astronauts, and a talking computer named HAL. The first twenty minutes, known as "The Dawn of Man," showed our apelike ancestors going through primitive daily life. One of the apes realizes a bone can be used as a tool. The scene captures a milestone in human evolution: the discovery of tools and technology. When the ape hurls the bone into the air, it turns, in slow motion, into a spacecraft.

"It is the longest cut in all of cinema: millions of years of human evolution in a single frame," writes Robert Poole in *History Today*. Suddenly, it's the year 2001, and the scene is a spaceship. *2001: A Space Odyssey*, writes Poole, "conveyed . . . the growing sense in the Sixties of the Space Age as a turning point in human history."

Apollo 8

By October 1968, it had been more than two years since NASA had sent men into space. That month, it launched *Apollo 7* astronauts Wally Schirra, Walt Cunningham, and Donn Eisele into orbit for eleven days. The astronauts brought aboard the first handheld video camera and put on a show for the folks on Earth. First, Schirra held up a card that read, "Hello from the lovely Apollo Room high atop everything." Eisele and Cunningham then performed gravity-free acrobatics, joyfully turning somersaults in midair as if celebrating the return of the United States to space. The mission was a success.

That November Richard M. Nixon was elected president, narrowly winning over Democrat Hubert Humphrey and third-party candidate George Wallace. The space program, which owed so much to the efforts of Kennedy and Johnson, had a new steward, President Richard Nixon.

The next Apollo mission, NASA announced, would orbit the Moon. Never before had humans left Earth's gravitational field. Every U.S. and Soviet launch had sent astronauts into Earth's orbit. This time human beings were going to go farther. On December 21, while

A Saturn rocket thunders from the launchpad, carrying *Apollo 8* into space on December 21, 1968. Aboard, astronauts Frank Borman, Jim Lovell, and William Anders considered their mission—orbiting the Moon.

Rising above the surface of the Moon, Earth emerges from the darkness of space. The *Apollo 8* astronauts took this image, "Earthrise," from lunar orbit.

much of the country was caught up in the rush of Christmas shopping, astronauts Frank Borman, Jim Lovell, and William Anders were blasted into space aboard *Apollo 8*.

When they entered lunar orbit, they became the first humans to see the back of the Moon with their own eyes. Using an on-flight camera, they shared the view with people on Earth. The Moon, said Lovell, "is a vastness of black and white—absolutely no color." So many meteorites had hit the Moon, Anders added, that "every square inch is pockmarked."

They were on the far side of the Moon when suddenly Borman cried out, "Look at that picture over there! Here's the Earth coming up!" It was an earthrise.

"Oh man, that's great," said Lovell. Anders caught the image on color film.

The photograph, called "Earthrise," became one of the most famous images of all time. In fact, the view of Earth, a beautiful blue and white ball alone in the darkness of space, appeared at a time when many people were eager to take better care of their planet. The "Earthrise" photograph captured their concerns in one vivid image.

Up until then, the U.S. government had passed only a handful of environmental laws. In the two years after *Apollo 8*, however, Congress passed the Clean Air Act; established the Environmental Protection Agency; and passed the National Environmental Policy Act of 1969 (NEPA), which set forth a national environmental policy "under which man and nature can exist in productive harmony." And in April 1970, just over a year later, the United States celebrated Earth Day, which became an annual event.

The *Apollo 8* astronauts were scheduled to be in lunar orbit on Christmas Eve. Surely that called for some sort of meaningful message.

The fiery *Apollo 8* space capsule streaks through Earth's atmosphere during re-entry in December 1968. In addition to carrying out their mission, the crew delivered a holiday message from space on Christmas Eve.

Divers and other recovery crew prepare to hoist the *Apollo 8* space capsule aboard the aircraft carrier U.S.S. *Yorktown* following splashdown in December 1968. The crew is already on the ship.

"We are now approaching lunar sunset," Anders announced that Christmas Eve, "and for all the people back on Earth, the crew of *Apollo 8* has a message that we would like to send to you." He began reading.

"In the beginning, God created the heaven and the Earth. And the Earth was without form, and void; and darkness was upon the face of the deep." He was reading from the first chapter of Genesis. Each astronaut took a turn reading from the biblical text. An airport bar near Houston went quiet as the astronauts' voices came over the television.

"And God saw that it was good," finished Borman. He paused a moment. "And from the crew of *Apollo 8,* we close with good night, good luck, a Merry Christmas, and God bless all of you—all of you on the good Earth."

Later, at home, Frank Borman remembers a telegram: "To the crew of *Apollo 8.* Thank you. You saved 1968."

The year was 1969, and NASA was ready to shoot for the Moon *(left)*.

"Fly Me to the Moon"

During the game, *Apollo 11* landed on the Moon. The announcers broke the news to the fans, and everyone broke into cheers and applause.

—Boston Red Sox fan, remembering the 1969 Moon landing

President Kennedy had set the goal for NASA: land a person on the Moon before the end of the decade. It was 1969, and NASA was right on schedule.

The Soviets were busy with their space agenda too. In January they accomplished the first manned docking of two Soviet spacecraft. Their engineers were known to be working on a huge rocket called the N-1, which was even bigger than the monster Saturn V rocket. But for what use was it intended? A lunar launch?

NASA moved forward with confidence, unaffected by Soviet doings. In March 1969, the agency successfully launched *Apollo 9*, with a command module named *Gumdrop* and a lunar module named *Spider*. Astronauts Jim McDivitt, Rusty Schweickart, and Dave Scott performed the first manned docking of the lunar module to the command module. In May astronauts Tom Stafford, Gene Cernan, and John Young of *Apollo 10*, in a command module named *Charlie Brown* and a lunar module named *Snoopy*, did everything the astronauts would do for the first lunar landing, except actually set the lunar module on the Moon. At the end of the *Apollo 10* mission, NASA's Chris Kraft remarked, "The practice is over. Next time we land."

Astronauts aboard the *Apollo 11* lunar module *Snoopy* photographed the command module *Charlie Brown (below)* as the module orbited 70 miles (113 km) above the Moon in May 1969.

The Soviet space program suffered an enormous setback in early July when their massive N-1 rocket exploded on the launchpad. If anyone had worried that the Soviets might somehow beat the Americans to the Moon, the explosion settled the question. Nobody but NASA was sending a crew to the Moon that month.

Opinion polls from that time showed that as much as half the U.S. population had doubts about the lunar landing. The public questioned the decision to spend so much money to go to the Moon when so many problems remained unsolved at home. Still, on July 16, 1969, as many as one million people gathered along the east coast of Florida to watch the launch of *Apollo 11* astronauts Neil Armstrong, Michael Collins, and Buzz Aldrin. The great journey that

The crew of *Apollo 11* peers out from the command module during a prelaunch inspection *(left)*. The men are *(from left to right)* Neil Armstrong, commander; Michael Collins, command module pilot; and Buzz Aldrin, lunar module pilot. *Apollo 11* lifts off *(right)* on July 16, 1969. The mission: a lunar landing.

Accompanied by Buzz Aldrin, Neil Armstrong pilots the *Apollo 11* lunar module, Eagle, toward the Moon's surface on July 20, 1969.

President Kennedy had spoken of so long ago was at hand.

The countdown began and then liftoff. "It was as if you could have stood on the dock and waved good-bye to Columbus," said CBS news anchor Walter Cronkite.

Four days later, the astronauts reached lunar orbit. Michael Collins, traveling in the *Columbia* command module, pulled away from the lunar module, *Eagle*, which would take Neil Armstrong and Buzz Aldrin to the Moon. "You cats take it easy on the lunar surface," Collins told them.

Armstrong prepared to land the lunar module on the Moon. Suddenly the computer's alarm bells sounded. Armstrong had to fly the module manually over a boulder field, all while running low on fuel.

All over the United States, all over the world, people were watching the Moon landing on TV. Abe and Ben Liss, who owned Beacon Television Rental in Washington, D.C., rented more than one thousand television sets that week. This was before the age of the VCR. Employers, hotel managers, hospital directors, and others rented TV sets for lobbies and waiting rooms so that people who couldn't be home could see the historic landing.

Interestingly, some NASA administrators initially opposed televising the Moon landing. A television camera, they argued, would add unnecessary weight to the capsule.

Chris Kraft of NASA would have none of it. "I can't believe what I'm hearing," he told his colleagues. "We've been looking forward to this flight—not just us, but the American taxpayers and, in fact, the whole world—since Kennedy put the challenge to us. Now you're willing to exclude the people of Earth from witnessing man's first steps on the Moon?"

So the astronauts brought a television camera. And all around the world, people watched as Neil Armstrong brought the lunar module onto the Moon's surface at 3:17 P.M. Houston time. "Houston, Tranquility Base here. The *Eagle* has landed," he said calmly.

"Roger, Tranquility," replied Charlie Duke at Mission Control. "We copy you on the ground. You got a bunch of guys about to turn blue. We're breathing again."

At Fenway Park in Boston, Massachusetts, home of the Boston Red Sox, the announcers gave a play-by-play account of the landing along with the play-by-play of the baseball game. When *Apollo 11* landed, "the announcers broke the news and everything stopped, the game, the fans, everyone—broke into cheers and applause!" said an anonymous fan.

At a department store in McLean, Virginia, someone called out, "We're landing!" Suddenly shoppers, clerks—a whole crowd—rushed to the TV department to watch. In Las Vegas casinos, blackjack games came to a halt. Kids at camp gathered around tiny sets in dining halls.

Lynda Van Devanter, an army nurse, was stationed at an army hospital in South Vietnam. "It had been a slow day and night in the [operating room]," she remembered, "so we all gathered around the small radio in the E.R. to listen. It was almost as if everyone, including the [Viet Cong], was so interested in the Moon landing that they had forgotten about the war." When the lunar module landed after 4 A.M. Saigon [Vietnam] time, she said, "a loud cheer went up throughout the . . . area and the sky filled with rockets, flares and fireworks."

At 3:17 P.M. Houston time on July 20, 1969, Neil Armstrong reported, "The *Eagle* has landed." Several hours later, the world watched transfixed as he descended *Eagle*'s ladder and took the first human steps on the surface of the Moon *(above)*.

Later that evening, the show got even better. Neil Armstrong was going to walk on the Moon.

In New York City's Central Park, the city had set up three huge television monitors. Thousands of people gathered to watch, and unlike so many crowds of that time, this one was upbeat and excited. They watched as Neil Armstrong, in a boxy white space suit, came out of the lunar module. "Live From the Moon," read the TV caption.

"I'm going to step off the LM [lunar module] now," he said. His big, white-booted foot came down on the Moon's surface. "That's one small step for a man, one giant leap for mankind," he said. The crowd in Central Park erupted in cheers.

Soon Buzz Aldrin came out of the lunar module. He and Armstrong set up a U.S. flag. They collected Moon rocks and samples of Moon dust. In the meantime, Michael Collins was orbiting the Moon alone, waiting for the two men's return.

Less than a day later, people again crowded around their television sets to watch the astronauts leave the Moon. The lunar module had just one engine. If it failed, Armstrong and Aldrin were in trouble.

"As *Eagle*'s lift-off time approached, I got really nervous," admitted Michael Collins. "If their engine didn't work, there was nothing I could do to rescue them from the surface. I simply had to come home by myself, leaving Neil and Buzz to die on the surface of the Moon."

Buzz Aldrin counted down the seconds to ignition. "Liftoff," he announced. The engine worked! The astronauts were on their way home! The *Eagle* soon docked with *Columbia*, and by July 24, all three astronauts were back on Earth.

Astronauts and lunar explorers Buzz Aldrin and Neil Armstrong insert the U.S. flag on the Moon's surface in 1969.

Aldrin sets up scientific equipment on the Moon's surface in 1969. In addition to their life-sustaining space suits, Aldrin and Armstrong wore weighted boots to help them overcome the low gravity of the Moon.

Six hundred million people from forty-seven countries are estimated to have watched the Moon landing. The journey of *Apollo 11* was "the greatest week in history since the Creation," said President Nixon.

And yet not everyone saw it. No matter how momentous an event, there will always be people who are too sick or sad to pay attention. Some simply aren't interested.

"We don't care about no Moon!" said a couple at a New York City bar when the bartender tried to switch the TV to *Apollo 11* coverage.

Madison Avenue Moon

When the *Apollo 11* astronauts returned to Earth, they remained under quarantine (in isolation) for more than two weeks in case they'd brought back "Moon germs." During quarantine, they ate

From zipper makers to frozen food producers, companies—including Stouffer's-capitalized on the the moon-landing mania to sell their products in the late 1960s.

Stouffer's frozen entrees and side dishes, including lobster Newburg, potatoes au gratin, and chicken and noodles. Stouffer's and NASA had worked for two years to come up with the selections, and the astronauts had given them their stamp of approval. Soon Stouffer's ads said, "Everybody who's been to the Moon is eating Stouffer's."

Space mania had been used to sell products for years. General Mills promoted Cheerios and V-8 vegetable juice as an "out of this world breakfast." The message confused at least one mother: she actually poured the V-8 onto the Cheerios. But advertisers had a field day with *Apollo 11*.

A Fritos commercial showed a lunar module landing on the Moon for the first time. The astronauts were greeted by none other than the Frito Bandito, the snack's cartoon mascot. "Welcome to the Moon, señor!" he said to the astronauts.

Talon, the zipper maker, pointed out in its advertisements that Talon was the first zipper on the Moon. Even Waldbaum's supermarkets got in on the act. One ad showing a picture of the Moon said, "238,000 miles from Waldbaum's. That's what we call brave. Imagine, being that far from our thick, fresh cottage cheese."

Kids who loved space didn't want cottage cheese. They wanted to eat and drink like astronauts. Until 1969 they had to settle for drinking Tang. Tang, the orange-flavored "instant breakfast drink," was first produced in the late fifties. When the public learned that the Gemini astronauts carried Tang on their missions, sales soared.

Then, the year of the Moon landing, Space Food Sticks arrived in supermarkets. Pillsbury had developed the chewy, high-energy snacks for the astronauts, then produced them for the public, packaging them in space-age silver wrappers. Available in flavors such as chocolate and peanut butter, they were the first energy bars.

The End of the Race

The race was over. The United States had beaten the Soviet Union. Of course, the Soviets claimed that they weren't even trying to get to the Moon. The truth didn't come out until much later, after the fall of Communism, that, in fact, they had been working toward a Moon landing after all.

Pillsbury made its Space Food Sticks—originally developed for astronauts—available to the public in 1969.

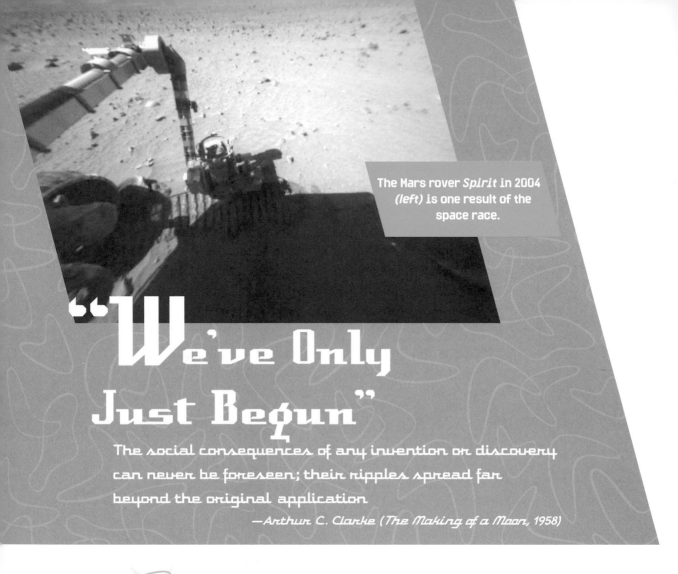

The Mars rover *Spirit* in 2004 *(left)* is one result of the space race.

"We've Only Just Begun"

The social consequences of any invention or discovery can never be foreseen; their ripples spread far beyond the original application

—Arthur C. Clarke (*The Making of a Moon*, 1958)

While the *Apollo 12* astronauts were rocketing into space in November 1969, thousands of the people who helped put them there—engineers, production workers, technicians—had been laid off from aerospace jobs. One man who had helped to train astronauts on the lunar module was managing a Tastee-Freez frozen custard stand. The aerospace industry was in a recession (economic downturn).

The American public's interest in space exploration had receded as well. When Alan Shepard was the first American in space, the whole country had cheered him on. In 1971 Shepard returned to space as the commander of *Apollo 14*. This time there was not one sign along the main roads of Cocoa Beach wishing the astronaut good luck.

The U.S. government, too, no longer treated space as a priority. Congress had recently canceled the planned *Apollo 18, 19,* and *20*. Too expensive, it said, and unnecessary since the United States already had beaten the Soviets to the Moon. What's more, fighting the Vietnam War created heavy strains on the federal budget, leaving little leftover cash for lunar roving. Finally, space travel was still risky. The *Apollo 13* astronauts had come close to dying when their spacecraft malfunctioned.

Apollo 13 astronaut John Swigert Jr. holds the "mailbox"—an air filter the crew built to purify the air in the spacecraft. The astronauts would not have survived their trip back to Earth in April 1970 without the improvised device.

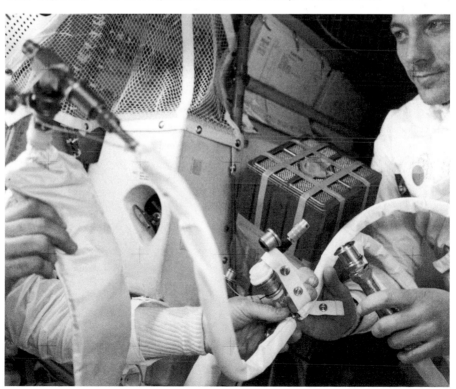

In December 1972, NASA launched *Apollo 17*, the last mission to the Moon. One Apollo mission remained, however, which could never have happened in the early days of the space race. In 1975 the United States and Soviet space programs launched the *Apollo-Soyuz* mission. Three American astronauts, including Deke Slayton (one of the original Mercury Seven), Tom Stafford, and Vance Brand, docked their *Apollo* spacecraft with the Soviet *Soyuz* and its two cosmonauts. They were Alexei Leonov, the first man to walk in space, and Valery Kubasov. While docked in space, the men exchanged seeds for planting

Apollo 17 astronaut Harrison H. Schmitt passes a bolder during a Moon walk in 1972. The landing team's lunar rover is in the foreground. The mission was the last to land anyone on the Moon. *Apollo 17* nears splashdown *(inset)*.

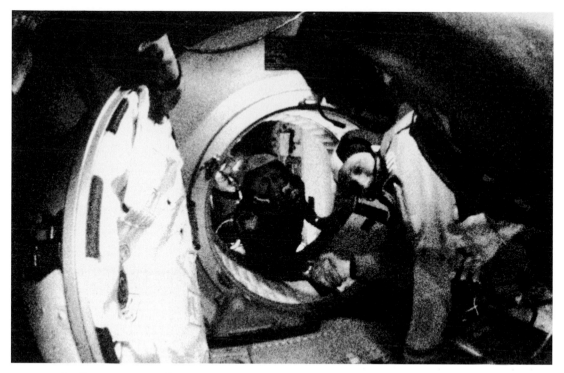

Apollo commander Thomas P. Stafford *(foreground)* and *Soyuz* commander Alexei A. Leonov make their historic handshake during the 1972 *Apollo-Soyuz* mission. The handshake took place in a docking module that joined the two craft.

trees in each other's countries upon their return. Astronaut Brand called it "a positive experience from beginning to end."

After Apollo

As the Apollo program ended, NASA turned its focus to projects closer to home. It launched *Skylab*, an experimental space station that orbited Earth from 1973 to 1979.

Then, in 1978, NASA chose a fresh group of thirty-five astronauts for its new Space Shuttle and International Space Station program. Shannon Lucid, the young woman who years earlier had written a letter to *Time* asking why all the Mercury Seven astronauts were men, was among this new group of astronauts. In fact, the group included six women, three African Americans, and an Asian. It also included

R. Mike Mullane, the kid who in the sixties had given up milk shakes in the hopes of going into space. Since then NASA's astronaut roster has grown ever more diverse.

Homer Hickam Jr., the "rocket boy" from Coalwood, West Virginia, eventually worked for NASA as an engineer. In fact, all the boys in the Big Creek Missile Agency went to college, "something not likely in pre-Sputnik West Virginia," wrote Hickam.

Stephen Lapekas, the Chicago teenager profiled in the 1961 *Life* magazine titled "Crisis in Education," joined the air force. He became a commercial pilot.

Edwinna Bernat, who early in her career had appreciated the new science materials she received after the launch of *Sputnik,* became an elementary school science teacher in Houston, Texas, and incorporated NASA's educational materials into her classroom. When her students conducted labs, she divided them into groups of four and gave each student a job, such as principal investigator and materials manager, just as they did at the space agency.

Stephen King, who heard about *Sputnik* while watching *Earth vs. the Flying Saucers*, became one of the best-selling horror novelists of all time. He credits the *Sputnik* incident as a major influence on his work.

End of the Cold War

And what of the Soviet Union? During the space race, the Soviet Union was the United States's number one enemy. By the late 1980s, it was on the verge of massive change. The Soviet leader, Mikhail Gorbachev, had begun reforms to strengthen the Soviet Union. These reforms allowed free elections in Eastern European countries.

First, the people of Poland elected a non-Communist government. Then, on the night of November 9, 1989, citizens of West and East Berlin began to tear down the Berlin Wall in a frenzy of excitement. In 1990 East and West Germany were reunited. One after another, Eastern European countries threw off the yoke of Soviet control.

With its giant solar panels *(top)* facing the Sun, the International Space Station hovers in low Earth orbit in the early 2000s. The station is a sixteen-country cooperative project to conduct space research.

Eventually, in 1991, the Communist Soviet Union buckled under the force of the reform movement. The Cold War was over.

The end of the Cold War has led to increased cooperation in space between NASA and the Russian space program. In the mid-1990s, NASA sent three astronauts to *Mir*, a Russian space station, via the space shuttle. One of the astronauts was Shannon Lucid, who stayed aboard *Mir* for 188 days, setting an endurance record for a woman in space. (*Mir* was "deorbited" in 2001.) The two countries went on to work together on the International Space Station (ISS). The International Space Station, a cooperative effort among sixteen nations, relies on spacecraft launched by both NASA and Russia to ferry supplies and crew members between Earth and the station.

Spinoffs

An earthling didn't have to follow the space race or even live through it to benefit from it. The space program brought about a huge number of technological achievements that have been incorporated into everyday products. Cordless power tools, for instance, started out as tools for extracting samples of the Moon's surface. When NASA scientists wanted to process signals from space into clearer pictures on their computers, they developed the technology now used by doctors in CAT scans (computer-aided tomography) and MRIs (magnetic resonance imaging). Water purification systems, scratch-resistant lenses, ear thermometers, TV satellite dishes, and virtual reality software all came from technology developed for the space program, as did the graphite used in golf clubs and the corrosion-resistant coating on the Statue of Liberty. And anyone who has ever used WD-40 to silence a squeaky door hinge has the space program to thank for it.

A NASA technician demonstrates a virtual hand device. The device, along with virtual reality software, allows users to control robots remotely.

The space race also played a role in the creation of the Internet. In 1958 President Eisenhower had established ARPA, the Advanced Research Projects Agency, as a direct response to *Sputnik*. In the mid-sixties, the folks at ARPA were looking for a way to communicate among computer systems at universities around the country that were engaged in ARPA-funded projects. They began working on what they called the ARPANET, or intergalactic network. On November 21, 1969, the first successful ARPANET link was established between computers at University of California in Los Angeles and Stanford University in California. ARPANET was the origin of the Internet.

Conspiracy Theory

In spite of its influence on so many lives, a few people began to say that NASA had never landed men on the Moon. The whole Moon landing, they said, had been faked. NASA had staged and filmed the entire thing rather than face global embarrassment by failing to carry out President Kennedy's mission.

Some people still think the Moon landing was staged. Some go so far as to say that NASA planned the *Apollo 1* disaster to keep astronaut Gus Grissom from exposing the hoax. In 2002 a man rushed *Apollo 11* astronaut Buzz Aldrin and his daughter as they tried to leave a hotel. Loudly calling Aldrin a liar and a fraud, the man shoved a stack of Bibles at him and demanded he swear that he had gone to the Moon. Aldrin, who risked his life to go to the Moon and had kept his cool during countless conspiracy accusations, punched him in the nose.

What's Next?

In recent years, NASA's manned space program has focused on the International Space Station and the space shuttle. No U.S. astronaut has traveled beyond low-Earth orbit (relatively close to the planet) since the end of the Apollo program. For longer journeys, NASA has relied on unmanned missions. Its many probes rove the galaxy. The probe, *Voyager 1*, launched in 1977, has flown past Jupiter, Saturn, Uranus, and Neptune, and is now approaching the outer reaches of the solar system.

Debate swirls over whether future missions should be manned or unmanned. Some experts say that it is cheaper and just as effective to send a robot to a distant planet than to undertake the risk and tremendous expense of sending humans. They point to the two space

This collage was created by NASA scientists, who put together images taken by *Voyager 1* of Jupiter *(back center)* and three of its moons.

A boy holds a Lego model of the space shuttle *Discovery* in 2005. Grounded since the 2003 *Columbia* re-entry disaster, the space shuttle returned to service in 2005.

shuttle missions that have ended in disaster: in 1986 the *Challenger* exploded soon after takeoff, and in 2003, the *Columbia* orbiter broke apart just sixteen minutes before landing. In both incidents, the entire crew perished. Advocates for manned exploration, on the other hand, stress that no machine can replace the powers of observation that a person brings to such a mission.

"In" Space

Many Americans who grew up during the space race are wondering what happened to all that futuristic stuff they had expected to see in the near future. They'd anticipated Moon colonies, interplanetary exploration, a car like George Jetson's!

Fans of the space age may lack space cars, but they have found other ways to indulge their enthusiasm. Space-age design, for instance, is popular again. Vintage furniture stores do a brisk business in pieces by Verner Panton, Eero Aarnio, and other sixties-era designers. Architectural preservationists in such places as Anaheim, California, and Wildwood, New Jersey, are working to save sixties-era buildings like the Satellite Motel from the wrecking ball. Even the Space Needle in Seattle, erected as part of the 1960 World's Fair, has been given a new purpose. It is home to the Science Fiction Museum and Hall of Fame.

Space-age popular culture has a solid fan base as well. Television shows such as *I Dream of Jeannie* and *The Jetsons* live on in reruns on cable TV. *Star Trek* fans gather for annual conventions, and the show has spawned movies and *Star Trek* spin-offs. Space toys are hot collectibles. Major Matt Mason and his accessories, for instance, sell well on online trading sites such as ebay. Even space-age food is back. Space Food Sticks, which had been discontinued, are back on the market thanks to adults who loved them as kids.

Built for the 1960s World's Fair, the Space Needle still stands in Seattle, Washington, as a monument to the space age.

Anchored to foot restraints, U.S. mission specialist Stephen K. Robinson rides the International Space Station's robotic arm to the space shuttle *Discovery* for exterior repairs in August 2005.

Looking to the Stars

Some people moan that the best days of space exploration ended with *Apollo 11*. Perhaps, however, the best days are ahead.

In September 2005, NASA unveiled plans to return to the Moon by 2018 as part of a program to eventually send people to Mars. The new mission would allow astronauts to live on the Moon for up to six months, creating a base and preparing for later trips to Mars.

Because of this, James L. Carter is making "Moon dirt" again. Back in the nineties, Carter, a geoscience professor, supplied NASA with 25 tons (23 metric tons) of fake "Moon dirt," which he grinds, according to a secret method, from volcanic ash so that it mirrors the properties of real Moon dirt. NASA has contacted him about a new supply. The agency will need fake Moon dirt to test how space suits and machinery function when coated or clogged with the dusty grime.

Future astronauts flock to U.S. Space Camp in Huntsville, Alabama. Here young space enthusiasts can try the Multi-Axis Trainer (MAT), which simulates a spinning space capsule, climb the Zero G (gravity) Wall, and bounce around in the One-Sixth Gravity Chair. Any modern kid can dream of going into space. In 1981 Jose Hernandez, the son of migrant farm workers, was laboring in a beet field when he heard on his radio that NASA had selected the first Latino astronaut, Franklin Chang-Diaz. Inspired, Hernandez decided to pursue a career in space, and in 2004, NASA selected him as an astronaut trainee.

Private companies are venturing into space as well. On June 21, 2004, Michael Melville flew *SpaceShipOne,* a private rocket plane designed by Burt Rutan, into space. It was the first time a private citizen, someone not affiliated with a national space program, had gone

NASA's rover *Spirit (partially visible at bottom)* took this image of the surface of Mars in 2005. Plans are in the works for further virtual exploration of the red planet and a possible manned mission there.

that far. Private companies are also developing creations like spacecraft powered by the light of the sun and rockets that hoist payloads (supplies) at less cost than government-funded ones.

In an office at NASA's Jet Propulsion Lab in Pasadena, California, Brian Cooper, a NASA engineer, is sitting in front of a computer carefully guiding his mouse. "It can't take it ennymore, Cap'n!" he exclaims, imitating Scotty from *Star Trek*. From his desk, he is "driving" the space rover, *Opportunity*, across the surface of Mars at the speed of 0.1 mile per hour (0.2 km per hour), trying to avoid a nasty-looking crater. Down the hall, another engineer "drives" *Spirit*, the other Mars rover. A sign on his office door reads, "My other cars are on Mars."

The remaining Mercury Seven astronauts still get fan mail every day. Near Kennedy Space Center, a T-shirt store sells a T-shirt emblazoned with a rocket launching over a U.S. flag. The shirt's message is simple. It says, "Keep the Dream Alive!"

Excerpt from *Apollo 11* Lunar Landing Communications

On July 16, 1969, Neil Armstrong, Buzz Aldrin, and Michael Collins blasted off for the Moon. On July 20, Armstrong and Aldrin landed *Eagle* (the lunar module) on the surface of the Moon. Below is part of the transcript of the conversations among Armstrong and Aldrin landing on the Moon's surface, Collins orbiting it in *Columbia* (the command module), and scientists at the Manned Space Center in Houston, Texas. The times at the left are measured in hours, minutes, and seconds from the original blastoff.

102:44:02 Armstrong: Okay. Here's a . . . Looks like a good area here.

102:44:04 Aldrin: I got the shadow out there.

102:44:07 Aldrin: 250, down at 2½, 19 forward. [Pause]

102:44:13 Aldrin: Altitude-velocity lights.

102:44:16 Aldrin: 3½ down, 220 feet, 13 forward. [Pause]

102:44:23 Aldrin: 11 forward. Coming down nicely.

102:44:25 Armstrong: Gonna be right over that crater. . . .

102:44:54 Aldrin: Okay. 75 feet. And it's looking good. Down a half, 6 forward.

. . .

102:45:31 Duke: 30 seconds.

102:45:32 Aldrin: Drifting forward just a little bit; that's good. [Garbled]

102:45:40 Aldrin: Contact light.

102:45:43 Armstrong: Shutdown.

102:45:44 Aldrin: Okay. Engine stop.

. . .

102:45:57 Duke: We copy you down, *Eagle.*

102:45:58 Armstrong: Engine arm is off. [Pause] Houston, Tranquility Base here. The *Eagle* has landed.

102:46:06 Duke: [Momentarily tongue-tied] Roger, Twan . . . [correcting himself] Tranquility. We copy you on the ground. You got a bunch of guys about to turn blue. We're breathing again. Thanks a lot.

102:46:16 Aldrin: Thank you.

102:46:18 Duke: You're looking good here.

102:46:23 Armstrong: Okay. [To Buzz] Let's get on with it. [To Houston] Okay. We're going to be busy for a minute.

. . .

109:15:45 Aldrin: Okay. About ready to go down and get some Moon rock?

109:15:47 Armstrong: My antenna's out. [Pause]

109:15:55 Armstrong: Now we're ready to hook up the LEC [or Lunar Equipment Conveyor that carried equipment from the lunar module to the surface] here. [Pause]

109:16:12 Aldrin: All right. That should go down with no twists now. Put the [LEC stowage] bag up this way. . . . Okay, are you hooked up to it?

109:16:26 Armstrong: Hmm? [Pause] Okay. Now we need to hook this . . .

109:16:30 Armstrong: Yeah. Move that up there.

109:16:34 Armstrong: Okay. [Pause] Okay. Your visor . . .

109:16:49 Aldrin: Okay. Your back is up against the purse. [Pause] All right. . . . Forward and up; now you are clear. Little bit toward me. [Pause] Straight down. To your left a little bit. Plenty of room. [Pause] Okay, you're lined up nicely. Toward me a little bit, down. Now you're clear. You're catching the first hinge. [Garbled]

109:17:26 Armstrong: The what hinge?

109:17:29 Aldrin: All right. Move . . . To your . . . Roll to the left. Okay. Now you're clear. You're lined up on the platform. Put your left foot to the right a little bit. Okay. That's good. Roll left. Good. [Pause]

109:17:54 Armstrong: Okay. Now I'm going to check ingress here. [Pause]

109:18:05 Aldrin: Okay. You're not quite squared away. Roll to the...Roll right a little. Now you're even.

...

109:19:16 Armstrong: Okay. Houston, I'm on the porch.

109:19:20 McCandless: Roger, Neil. [Long Pause]

109:19:36 Aldrin: Okay. Stand by, Neil.

109:19:37 McCandless: *Columbia. Columbia.* This is Houston....All systems Go. Over.

109:19:46 Collins: *Columbia.* Thank you.

109:19:47 Aldrin: Stay where you are a minute, Neil.

109:19:48 Armstrong: Okay. Need a little slack? [No answer; Long Pause] You need more slack, Buzz?

109:20:40 Aldrin: No. Hold it just a minute.

109:20:41 Armstrong: Okay. [Long Pause]

109:20:56 Aldrin: Okay. Everything's nice and straight in here.

109:20:58 Armstrong: Okay. Can you pull the door open a little more?

109:21:00 Aldrin: All right.

109:21:03 Armstrong: Okay. [Pause]

109:21:22 McCandless: This is Houston. Roger. We copy. Standing by for your TV.

109:21:39 Armstrong: Houston, this is Neil. Radio check.

109:21:42 McCandless: Neil, this is Houston. Loud and clear. Break. Break. Buzz, this is Houston. Radio check, and verify TV circuit breaker in.

109:21:54 Aldrin: Roger, TV circuit breaker's in. And read you loud and clear.

109:22:00 McCandless: Roger. [Pause]

109:22:06 McCandless: And we're getting a picture on the TV!

109:22:09 Aldrin: You got a good picture, huh?

109:22:11 McCandless: There's a great deal of contrast in it; and currently it's upside-down on our monitor, but we can make out a fair amount of detail.

109:22:28 Aldrin: Okay. Will you verify the position—the opening—I ought to have on the [16 mm movie] camera?

109:22:34 McCandless: Stand by. [Long Pause]

109:22:48 McCandless: Okay. Neil, we can see you [on the TV] coming down the ladder now. [Pause]

109:22:59 Armstrong: Okay. I just checked getting back up to that first step, Buzz. It's . . . The strut isn't collapsed too far, but it's adequate to get back up.

109:23:10 McCandless: Roger. We copy.

109:23:11 Armstrong: Takes a pretty good little jump [to get back up to the first rung]. [Pause]

109:23:25 McCandless: Buzz, this is Houston. F/2 [camera setting] . . .

109:23:28 Armstrong: Okay, I'm at the . . . [Listens]

109:23:29 McCandless: 1/160th second for shadow photography on the sequence camera.

109:23:35 Aldrin: Okay.

109:23:38 Armstrong: I'm at the foot of the ladder. The LM [Lunar Module] footpads are only depressed in the surface about 1 or 2 inches, although the surface appears to be very, very fine grained, as you get close to it. It's almost like a powder. [The] ground mass is very fine. [Pause]

109:24:13 Armstrong: I'm going to step off the LM now. [Long Pause]

109:24:48 Armstrong: That's one small step for [a] man; one giant leap for mankind.

This transcript of the *Apollo 11* lunar landing communications is courtesy of Eric Jones and NASA, http://www.hq.nasa.gov/alsj. Used by permission.

Visit *Apollo 11* Multimedia, http://www.hq.nasa.gov/office/pao/History/alsj/a11/video11.html, for video and audio clips from the lunar landing.

Timeline

1957 October 4: Soviet Union launches *Sputnik 1.*
November 3: Soviet Union launches *Sputnik 2* with Laika, a dog, aboard.
December 6: A U.S. Vanguard rocket test fails.

1958 January 31: The United States launches *Explorer 1.*
October 1: NASA is established.
December 18: Project SCORE communications satellite is launched.

1959 April: NASA introduced first seven astronauts.
July: U.S. president Richard Nixon and Soviet premier Nikita Khrushchev
hold the Kitchen Debate in Moscow.
September 12: The Soviet probe *Luna 2* reaches the Moon.

1960 August 18: *Echo 1,* a U.S. communications satellite, relays first message
from space.
August 19: Soviets launch *Sputnik 5* with two dogs aboard.

1961 January 31: NASA launches Ham, a chimpanzee, into space.
April 12: Soviets launch first person, Yuri Gagarin, into space.
May 5: Alan Shepard in *Freedom 7* is first U.S. astronaut sent into space.
July 21: Gus Grissom, in *Liberty Bell,* is second American in space.
August 6: Gherman Titov, in *Vostok 2,* orbits Earth seventeen times.

1962 February 20: American John Glenn orbits Earth three times.
May 24: Scott Carpenter orbits Earth three times.
August: Soviet Union launches two spacecraft with Andrian Nikolayev
and Pavel Popovitch aboard.
October: Wally Schirra of the United States orbits Earth six times.

1963 May 15: American Gordon Cooper lifts off in *Faith 7* and orbits Earth 22 times.
June 16: Soviets send first woman, Valentina Tereshkova, into space.

1964 October 12: Soviets launch three men in *Voskhod 1.*

1965 March: Soviets launch two-man *Voskhod 2.*
March : The United States launches *Gemini 3* with John Young and
Gus Grissom aboard.
June 3: *Gemini 4* is launched with Jim McDivitt and Ed White aboard. White
is the first American to walk in space.
August: Gordon Cooper and Pete Conrad spend eight days in space in *Gemini 5.*
December: Wally Schirra and Tom Stafford in *Gemini 6* meet up with
Jim Lovell and Frank Borman in *Gemini 7.*

1966 March: The United States launches *Gemini 8* with Neil Armstrong
and Dave Scott aboard.
May: U.S. probe *Surveyor 1* lands on Moon.
September: *Gemini 12,* with Jim Lovell and Buzz Aldrin, is final Gemini mission.

1967 January 27: A fire in *Apollo 1* capsule kills Gus Grissom, Ed White,
and Roger Chaffee.
April: Soviet cosmonaut Vladimir Komarov is killed in re-entry accident.
November: NASA launches an unmanned Saturn-V rocket.

1968 October: *Apollo 7,* with Wally Schirra, Walt Cunningham, and Donn Eisele
aboard, carries first video camera.
December 21: *Apollo 8* is launched with Frank Borman, Jim Lovell,
and William Anders aboard.

1969 March: Jim McDivitt, Rusty Schweickart, and Dave Scott successfully dock
lunar module to command module on *Apollo 9.*
May: *Apollo 10* astronauts jim Stafford, Gene Cernan, and Young successfully
dock modules.
July: A Soviet N-1 rocket explodes on the launchpad.
July 16: *Apollo 11* heads to the Moon with Neil Armstrong, Michael Collins,
and Buzz Aldrin aboard.
July 20: The *Eagle,* the lunar module, lands on the Moon, and Armstrong
and Aldrin explore the Moon's surface.
November 19: *Apollo 12* astronauts Charles Conrad and Alan Bean walk
on the Moon.

1970 April 11: *Apollo 13*'s Jim Lovell, Fred Haise, and John Swigert survive
an explosion in the spacecraft while in space.

1971 February 5: *Apollo 14* LM, with Shepard and Edgar D. Mitchell aboard, lands
on the Moon.
July 30: David Scott and James Irwin in *Apollo 15* drive on the Moon's surface.

1972 April 21: *Apollo 16* LM, with Charles Duke and John Young aboard, lands on
the Moon. Thomas Mattingly pilots the command module.
December 11: *Apollo 17,* with Gene Cernan and Harrison Schmitt aboard, is
the final Moon mission.

1975 July 17: *Apollo-Soyuz* mission: *Apollo,* with astronauts Thomas Stafford, Deke
Slayton, and Vance Brand aboard, docks with the Soviet *Soyuz,* manned by
Alexi Leonov and Valery Kubasov.

7 Stephen King, *Danse Macabre* (New York: Berkley Books, 1981), n.p.

8 Homer H. Hickam Jr., *October Sky* (New York: Delacorte Press, 1998), 18.

8 Ibid., 19.

9–10 "Panic Is a Worse Enemy than 'Dirty' Bombs," *Los Angeles Times,* June 12, 2002.

11 "Bomb Shelter Bill Does Foreign Policy," *Weekly Standard,* December 13, 1999.

11 Pam Miller, conversation with author, October 28, 2004.

11 Ibid.

11–12 R. Mike Mullane, *Liftoff! An Astronaut's Dream* (Parsippany, NJ: Silver Burdett Press, 1995), 61–62.

12 Paul Dickson, *Sputnik: The Shock of the Century* (New York: Walker and Co., 2001), 62.

12 Hickam, 20.

12 "Conversation with Eilene Galloway," in *Legislative Origins of the National Aeronautics and Space Act of 1958: Proceedings of an Oral History Workshop Conducted April 3, 1992,* http://www.hq.nasa.gov/office/pao/History/40thann/legislat.pdf (December 2005).

12 United Press, "Official White House Transcript of President Eisenhower's Press and Radio Conference No. 123, October 9, 1957," in *Sputnik Documents,* n.d., http://www.eisenhower.utexas.edu/dl/Sputnik/Sputnikdocuments.html (December 2005).

12 Ibid., 8.

16 NASA/Jet Propulsion Laboratory, "A 70,000-Carat U.S. Space 'Gem' Marks Its Sapphire Anniversary," news release, January 31, 2003.

16 Hickam, 90.

18 Stephen Lapekas, "Crisis in Education," *Life,* March 24, 1958, 33.

19 Alexi Kutzhov, "Crisis in Education," *Life,* March 24, 1958, 27.

19 Ibid., 30.

19 Sloan Wilson, "Crisis in Education," *Life,* March 24, 1958, 37.

21 "Conversation with Willis Shapley," in *Legislative Origins of the National Aeronautics and Space Act of 1958.*

21 Stewart E. McClure, "Oral History Transcript of Interview No. 4, January 28, 1983," in *U.S. Senate Historical Office Oral History Project,* n.d., http://www.senate.gov/history (December 2005).

21 Ibid.

22 Peter Dow, "Sputnik Revisited: Historical Perspectives on Science Reform," *Sputnik Revisited,* 1997, http://www.nas.edu/sputnik/dow2.htm (December 2005).

23 Hickam, 91.

24 Mullane, 62.

24 "Conversation with Paul G. Dembling," in *Legislative Origins of the National Aeronautics and Space Act of 1958.*

24 "Conversation with Eilene Galloway," in *Legislative Origins of the National Aeronautics and Space Act of 1958.*

25 *SCORE (Signal Communication by Orbiting Relay Equipment),* 2005, http://www.globalsecurity.org/space/systems/score.htm (December 2005).

26 Mullane, 65.

26 Hillary Rodham Clinton, *Living History* (New York: Simon and Schuster, 2003), 20.

26–27 CNN, *Nikita Khrushchev and Richard Nixon (Debate, Moscow, USSR, July 24, 1959),* 2005,

http://edition .cnn.com/
SPECIALS/cold.war/episodes/14/
documents/debate (December
2005).

27 Ibid.

27–28 Hickam, 390.

29 Hugh Sidey, *John F. Kennedy,
President* (New York: Atheneum,
1963), 113.

30–31 "Kennedy Declares Castro Is
Enemy; Sees U.S. Arms Lag," *New
York Times,* August 27, 1960.

31 Sidey, 113.

31 John F. Kennedy (campaign speech,
Do Drop Inn, Muskegon, MI,
September 5, 1960), *JFK Link,*
n.d., available online at http://www
.jfklink.com/speeches/jfk/sept60/
jfk050960_musk02.html
(December 2005).

32 John F. Kennedy, "Inaugural
Address, Washington, DC, January
20, 1961," *John F. Kennedy Library
and Museum,* 2005, http://
www.jfklibrary.org/j012061.htm
(December 2005).

34 Chris Kraft, *Flight: My Life in
Mission Control* (New York:
Penguin, 2001), 131.

34 "Thousands March in Moscow to
Cheer Man-in-Space Flight," *New
York Times,* April 13, 1961.

35 Sidey, 119.

35 Ibid., 120.

36 Jay Gold, ed., *To the Moon* (New
York: Time-Life Records, 1969), 55.

36 Hugh Sidey, "A Great Quest Takes
Its Toll," *Time,* February 10, 2003,
90.

36 Robert Conley, "Nation Exults over
Space Feat; City Plans to Honor
Astronaut," *New York Times,* May
6, 1961.

36 Kraft, 139.

37 John F. Kennedy, "Special Message to
the Congress on Urgent National
Needs, May 25, 1961," *NASA Office of
Logic and Design,* 2005, http://
www.klabs.org/richcontent/speeches/
kennedyspeech.htm (May 2005).

37 Kraft, 143.

39 John Glenn, *Letters to John Glenn,*
with J. H. Glenn Jr. (Houston:
World Book Encyclopedia Service,
1964), 29.

39 Ibid.

39 Ibid., 35.

39 P. L. Prattis, "I'm Fenced Out," *New
Pittsburgh Courier,* March 10, 8.

40 John Glenn, *John Glenn: A Memoir,*
with Nick Taylor (New York: Bantam
Books, 1999), 290.

40 Robert Zimmerman, *Genesis: The
Story of* Apollo 8 (New York: Avalon,
1998), 104.

41 John F. Kennedy (speech, Rice
Stadium, Houston, TX, September
12, 1962), *University of Massachusetts,*
2005, available online at http://
www.cs.umb.edu/jfklibrary/j091262
.htm (December 2005).

42 Kraft, 176.

43 Steve Jobs, "Excerpts from an Oral
History Interview with Steve Jobs,
Founder of NeXT Computer, and
Cofounder of Apple Computer, April
20, 1995," *Interview with Steve Jobs
(Part 1),* 2003, http:// www.geocities
.com/franktau/interviewpart1.html
(December 2005).

44 "America's 6,000-Mile Walk in
Space," *National Geographic,*
September 1965, 447.

45 Gregory Lawrence, interview with
the author, February 2005.

46 Cara Greenberg, *Op to Pop: Furniture
of the 1960s* (Boston: Little, Brown,
1999), 26–27.

47 Shelby Grad, *Googie Architecture,* n.d., http://www.anaheimcolony .com/googie.htm (December 2005).

47 James Schefter, *The Race: The Complete True Story of How America Beat Russia to the Moon* (Garden City, NY: Doubleday, 1999), 192.

47 Ibid.

48 Martha Ackmann, *The Mercury 13: The Untold Story of Thirteen American Women and the Dream of Space Flight* (New York: Random House, 2003), 132.

48 Mary Finch Hoyt, *American Women of the Space Age* (New York: Atheneum, 1966), 43.

48 Gold, 70.

49 Robert B. Semple Jr., ed., *Four Days in November: The Original Coverage of the JFK Assassination by the Staff of the* New York Times (New York: St. Martin's Press, 2003), 80.

52 Robert R. Gilruth, "The Making of an Astronaut," *National Geographic,* January 1965, 122.

53 Martin Luther King Jr., "'I Have a Dream' Speech, Delivered at the March on Washington for Jobs and Freedom, Washington, D.C., August 28, 1963," *Martin Luther King Jr. Papers Project at Stanford University,* 2005, http://www.stanford.edu/ group/King/popular_requests (December 2005).

54 Alvin J. Bronstein, e-mail message to the author, October 25, 2002.

54 Kraft, 214.

55 Tom D. Crouch, *Aiming for the Stars: The Dreamers and Doers of the Space Age* (Washington, DC: Smithsonian Institution Press, 1999), 194.

55 Schefter, 211.

55 Kraft, 217.

55 Ibid., 222.

56 Ibid., 225.

56 "*Star Trek* Tidbits," *The Fifties Web,* n.d., http://www.fiftiesweb .com/tv/star-trek.htm (December 2005).

57 "When *Star Trek* Was New" video interview with William Shatner, September 1966, n.d., http://www .trek5.com/video/1966__interviews (December 2004).

58 Frank Borman, *Countdown: An Autobiography,* with Robert J. Serling (New York: William Morrow, 1988), 220.

58 Mark Salzman, *Lost in Place: Growing up Absurd in Suburbia* (New York: Random House, 1995), 14–18.

59 Schefter, 227.

59 Kraft, 244.

61 Schefter, 236.

63 Ibid., 247.

64 Walter Cronkite, *A Reporter's Life* (New York: Random House, 1996), 279.

64 Sears Roebuck Co., *1967 Wishbook,* (Chicago: Sears Roebuck Co., 1967), 495.

65 Cyberqat 1963 (user), "Personal Memory, Added October 30, 2003," n.d., *Feeling Retro,* http://www .feelingretro.com (December 2004).

67 Hugh Sidey, "A Great Quest Takes Its Toll," *Time,* February 10, 2003, 90.

67 Robert Poole, "2001: A Space Odyssey," *History Today,* January 2001, 39.

69 Zimmerman, 243.

69 Ibid.

69 Ibid., 199.

69 Ibid.

70 "National Environmental Policy Act of 1969, Title 1, Sec. 101(a)," *NEPA of 1969,* n.d., http://ceq .eh .doe.gov/nepa/regs/nepa/ nepaeqia .htm (December 2005).

71 Zimmerman, 244.

71 Ibid., 245.

71 Ibid., 246.

71 Borman, 220.

72 C. M. Pate, "Stories of the Most Amazing Day on Earth: July 20, 1969," *Where Were You?* 1999, http://wherewereyou.com/frames/ public.html (December 2005).

73 Kraft, 310.

75 Joe Garner, *Stay Tuned: Television's Unforgettable Moments* (Kansas City, MO: Andrews McMeel, 2002), 78.

75 Michael Collins, *Carrying the Fire: An Astronaut's Journey* (New York: Farrar, Straus, 1974), 403.

76 Kraft, 308.

76 "Transcript of *Apollo 11* Tape 66/12, 317," *Apollo Lunar Surface Journal,* n.d., http://history.nasa .gov/alsj/ a11.html (December 2005).

76 Ibid.

76 Lynda Van Devanter, *Home Before Morning* (New York: Warner/Beaufort, 1983), 124.

76 Ibid.

76 *Where Were You July 20, 1969?* 1999, http://www.wherewereyou .com (December 2005).

77 "Transcript of *Apollo 11,* Tape 70/24," *Apollo Lunar Surface Journal,* n.d., http://history.nasa.gov .alsj/ a11.html (December 2005).

78 Michael Collins, *Flying to the Moon and Other Strange Places* (New York: Farrar, Straus, 1976), 136.

79 Michael Browning, Knight-Ridder /Tribune News Service, "What We Did in 1969, We Probably Could Not Do Again Today," *Highbeam Research,* 1994, http://www.highbeam.com/static .highbeam.com/k/ knightriddertribunenewsservice/ july171994 (December 2005).

80 User comment, 2004, http://www .archive.org/movies/details-db.php ?collection+prelinger&collectionid +0578 (February 2004).

82 Arthur C. Clarke, "The Making of a Moon," in Donald Cox and Michael Stoiko, *Spacepower: What it Means to You* (Philadelphia: John C. Winston, 1958), 94.

85 Jay Levine, "Brand Recalls *Apollo-Soyuz* Mission," *Dryden X-Press,* August 25, 2001.

86 Hickam, 422.

95 Joel Achenbach, "Plan 1 for Outer Space," *Washington Post,* August 29, 2004, D1.

Selected Bibliography

Ackmann, Martha. *The Mercury 13: The Untold Story of Thirteen American Women and the Dream of Space Flight.* New York: Random House, 2003.

Aldrin, Buzz, and Wendell Minor. *Reaching for the Moon.* New York: HarperCollins, 2005.

Archer, Jules. *The Incredible Sixties: The Stormy Years That Changed America.* San Diego: Harcourt, Brace, Jovanovich, 1986.

Briggs, Carol S. *Women in Space.* Minneapolis: Lerner Publications Company, 1999.

Cole, Michael D. *Friendship 7: First American in Orbit.* Berkeley Heights, NJ: Enslow Publishers, 1995.

———. *Space Launch Disaster: When Liftoff Goes Wrong.* Berkeley Heights, NJ: Enslow Publishers, 2000.

Dickson, Paul. *Sputnik: The Shock of the Century.* New York: Walker and Co., 2001.

Dow, Peter B. *Schoolhouse Politics: Lessons from the Sputnik Era.* Cambridge, MA.: Harvard University Press, 1991.

Glenn, John. *John Glenn: A Memoir.* With Nick Taylor. New York: Bantam Books, 1999.

Greenberg, Cara. *Op to Pop: Furniture of the 1960's.* Boston: Little, Brown and Company, 1999.

Hafner, Katie, and Matthew Lyon. *Where Wizards Stay Up Late: The Origins of the Internet.* New York: Simon and Schuster, 1996.

Harford, James. *Korolev: How One Man Masterminded the Soviet Drive to Beat America to the Moon.* New York: John Wiley and Sons, 1997.

Hickam, Homer H., Jr. *Rocket Boys.* New York: Delacorte Press, 1998.

Kevles, Bettyann Holtzmann. *Almost Heaven: The Story of Women in Space*. New York: Basic Books, 2003.

Kraft, Chris. *Flight: My Life in Mission Control*. New York: Penguin, 2001.

Mullane, R. Mike. *Liftoff! An Astronaut's Dream*. Parsippany, NJ: Silver Burdett Press, 1995.

Phelps, J. Alfred. *They Had a Dream: The Story of African-American Astronauts*. Novato, CA: Presidio, 1994.

Schefter, James. *The Race: The Complete True Story of How America Beat Russia to the Moon*. Garden City, NY: Doubleday, 1999.

Schyffert, Bea Uusma. *The Man Who Went to the Far Side of the Moon*. San Francisco: Chronicle Books, 2003.

Stott, Carole. *Moon Landing: The Race for the Moon*. New York: DK Publishing, 1999.

Thompson, Neal. *Light This Candle: The Life and Times of Alan Shepard —America's First Spaceman*. New York: Crown, 2004.

Topham, Sean. *Where's My Space Age? The Rise and Fall of Futuristic Design*. Munich, Germany: Prestel Publishing, 2003.

Zimmerman, Robert. *Genesis: The Story of* Apollo 8. New York: Avalon Publishing Group, 1998.

Further Reading and Websites

Anderson, Catherine Corley. *John F. Kennedy.* Minneapolis: Lerner Publications Company, 2004.

Briggs, Carol S. *Women in Space.* Minneapolis: Lerner Publications Company, 1999.

Butts, Ellen R., and Joyce R. Schwartz. *Fidel Castro.* Minneapolis: Lerner Publications Company, 2005.

Collins, Michael. *Flying to the Moon: An Astronaut's Story.* 2nd ed. New York: Farrar, Straus and Giroux, 1994.

Darby, Jean. *Dwight D. Eisenhower.* Minneapolis: Lerner Publications Company, 2004.

Finlayson, Reggie. *We Shall Overcome: The History of the American Civil Rights Movement.* Minneapolis: Lerner Publications Company, 2003.

Gottfried, Ted. *The Cold War.* Minneapolis: Lerner Publications Company, 2003.

Levy, Debbie. *Lyndon B. Johnson.* Minneapolis: Lerner Publications Company, 2003.

———. *The Vietnam War.* Minneapolis: Twenty-First Century Books, 2004.

Manheimer, Ann S. *Martin Luther King Jr.: Dreaming of Equality.* Minneapolis: Lerner Publications Company, 2005.

Márquez, Herón, *Richard M. Nixon.* Minneapolis: Lerner Publications Company, 2003.

NASA
http://www.nasa.gov
The official website of the National Aeronautics and Space Administration contains the latest information on current NASA missions, the history of NASA, as well as links to Web pages for students. The site also contains contact information and much more. Visit *NASA Image*

Exchange (NIX) http://nix.ksc.nasa.gov and *Great Images in NASA (GRIN)* http://grin.hq.nasa.com for mission photo histories.

NASA Mars Exploration Rover Mission
http://marsrovers.jpl.nasa.gov/home/index.html
This official website of NASA's Mars rover missions offers up-to-date information on the rovers *Spirit* and *Opportunity.*

Richardson, Hazel. *How to Build a Rocket.* New York: Franklin Watts, 2001.

Sherman, Josepha. *The Cold War.* Minneapolis: Twenty-First Century Books, 2004.

Smithsonian National Air and Space Museum
http://www.nasm.si.edu
The official website of the National Air and Space Museum boasts the largest collection of historic spacecraft and aircraft, as well as information, photographs, and illustrations.

The Space Race
http://www.thespacerace.com
This website is dedicated to the Mercury, Gemini, and Apollo space programs and provides videos, audio recordings, and photographs.

Streissguth, Tom. *John Glenn.* Minneapolis: Lerner Publications Company, 2005.

————. *Rocket Man: The Story of Robert Goddard.* Minneapolis: Lerner Publications Company, 1995.

Vogt, Gregory L. *Apollo Moonwalks: The Amazing Lunar Missions.* Berkeley Heights, NJ: Enslow Publishers, 2000.

————. *Disasters in Space Exploration.* rev. ed. Minneapolis: Lerner Publications Company, 2003.

Acknowledgments

The images in this book are used with the permission of: NASA Headquarters – GReatest Images of NASA, pp. 2, 8, 15, 32, 69, 83; © Francis Miller/Time Life Pictures/Getty Images, p. 6; © CORBIS, pp. 7, 27; © Bettmann/CORBIS, pp. 9, 30, 47, 49, 73, 77; © Pictorial Parade/Getty Images, p. 10; NASA, p. 13; NASA Marshall Space Flight Center, pp. 16, 17, 25, 34, 68, 87, 88; © Yale Joel/Time Life Pictures/Getty Images, p. 18; © Howard Sochurek & Stan Wayman/Life Magazine/Time & Life Pictures/Getty Images, p. 19; © Robert W. Kelley/Time Life Pictures/Getty Images, p. 23; © Stan Wayman/Time Life Pictures/Getty Images, p. 28; NASA Goddard Space Flight Center, p. 29; NASA Kennedy Space Center, pp. 33, 36, 39, 44, 63, 74 (both); NASA Johnson Space Center, pp. 38, 41, 56, 58, 60, 61, 70, 71, 75, 79, 84 (both), 85; © AFP/Getty Images, p. 42; © Hulton Archive/Getty Images, pp. 45, 51, 57; © Lipnitzki/Roger Viollet/Getty Images, p. 46; National Archives, p. 53; © Joseph Louw/Time Life Pictures/Getty Images, p. 66; PhotoDisc Royalty Free by Getty Images, p. 72; © NASA/Roger Ressmeyer/CORBIS, p. 78; This photo is made available as a courtesy by Nestle USA, p. 80; Courtesy of General Mills Archives, p. 81; NASA Jet Propulsion Laboratory, pp. 82, 90, 96 (background), 99 (background); © David McNew/Getty Images, p. 91; © Crady Von Pawlak/Hulton Archive/Getty Images, p. 92; © NASA/Getty Images, p. 93; NASA/JPL-Caltech/Cornell, p. 94.

Front Cover: NASA Johnson Space Center (left); NASA Kennedy Space Center (center); © Bettmann/CORBIS (right).

Titles from the AWARD-WINNING People's History Series

For more information, please call 1-800-328-4929 or visit www.lernerbooks.com